One Business, One Million, One Year!

The true story of a new technology start-up
going sky high very quickly and back down
even quicker!

Disclaimer

This story is based on actual events which are solely my personal views and recollections of what happened and how I feel things were handled.

The names of every person connected with my story have been changed to protect the privacy of these individuals.

Although I have made every effort to ensure that the information in this book is correct at press time, I do not assume and hereby disclaim any liability to any party for any loss, damage, or disruption caused by errors or omissions, whether such errors or omissions result from negligence, accident, or any other cause.

Foreword

It has been two years since the company I created with a colleague went into administration. At first, I felt a lot of anger and resentment at that failure, but now, two years on, I feel ready to write about this amazing experience.

I'm a software developer by trade, so I'm not the type of person to write books. However, I wanted to document those 12 insane months, both so that I have a written memory of everything that happened and also to share with you the events and opportunities we experienced. Reading this book may help you make decisions in your business, or maybe you too have faced business failure, have been hit hard, or are facing difficult life or business situations that relate in some way to chapters in this book. Or, read on simply for fun to discover the roller coaster of a year we had!

This book is to share my amazing experience of creating a business at the dawn of the virtual reality revolution, being offered a huge financial investment that the majority of start-ups can only dream of, travelling the world to showcase our products, meeting some amazing people from some of the largest corporations around and being offered some of the most incredible opportunities we would have never thought possible. And yet, during most of that time, we never stood a chance of succeeding. I know it sounds incredible, but I kid you not. In one of the last chapters, I will explain why from the very early days, the company was setting itself up to fail – and yet we had all the ingredients to make it a roaring success!

So, who am I? Well, as mentioned before, I have been a software developer for over 20 years and a freelance developer for the last 16 years. I've always considered myself a small entrepreneur in a way where I never had dreams of launching the next worldwide disruptive idea, but I have always liked tech and have taken every opportunity to develop products and business ideas using the latest trends.

Back in 2004, I launched a product that used biometric identification to sign in securely when, at the time, biometric identification was barely known.

A few years later, I followed the smartphone app revolution and started to develop several apps including a very early taxi app before Uber had been invented. Back in 2013, I launched one of the very few augmented reality apps for the Jersey Heritage Museum and then I started a virtual reality company.

When I started this new virtual reality company, I didn't anticipate how hard it was going to be. From the countless hours worked at the studio, often until 2 or 3am after an already full day; the numerous trips across the world; the board meeting arguments and the financial difficulties; the stressful administration processes; the opportunities to work on brand new technologies; showcasing our products across the world from Shanghai to Silicon Valley; and having more opportunities than you can shake a stick at, I believe my story has all the ingredients to be a Hollywood movie!

I also feel it's necessary to specify that I have written this book essentially from memories, but these are backed up by a copy of all our board meeting minutes and hundreds of emails. I'm pretty sure that some of the paragraphs are so extreme you may wonder if I am making things up, but I can assure you that while the views about certain people and decisions expressed in this book are mine, the facts and events are all genuine and actually happened.

The funny thing is, I ask myself sometimes, "Would I do it again?", and the answer is, "Yes" – but I would do so many things differently. Obviously, in hindsight, we would all do a number of things differently, but the simple reason why I would have no hesitation to do it all again is because I learned a lot during that time, not only about business, but about people and about myself – and that experience is so invaluable in my life now.

On a last note, like many other entrepreneurs, this business ruled my life for the best part of 15 months. It took me away from home a lot, it generated a lot of stress and pressure and ended with much anger and personal financial difficulties – so I thank my wife and my son for being there during that time. They have been two rocks I could hold onto when I could no longer see the daylight and when things seemed to be overwhelming. They have been very accommodating in supporting me when I was away during that time. So thank you guys. I love you!

CONTENTS

CHAPTER ONE

The start

It's early 2014. I'm meeting Paul at Costa Coffee as a chance encounter put together by a mutual friend. In the last three years, I've essentially been developing smartphone apps, one of which is an augmented reality (AR) app for a local museum which allows users to visualise the museum's artefacts on their phone or tablet in AR. After a couple of coffees, Paul and I quickly clicked and realised that we had a common interest in virtual reality (VR) although the technology is in its early days.

From now on in this book, I'll be using the common shorthand terms of AR to refer to augmented reality and VR to refer to virtual reality.

It's only been 18 months since Palmer Luckey raised $2.5million with his Oculus Rift Kickstarter campaign. I was one of the backers and I received my DK1 – Oculus' first ever VR headset, released as a result of the Kickstarter campaign – only a few months ago. As a self-confessed technology geek, I'm very keen to explore what VR can do and where it is going to take us. Paul, with his more technical background, is equally enthusiastic about VR. We complete each other; I'm the "softy" – or software developer and Paul is the "hardy" – or the hardware and technical guy. My skills end where Paul's skills start and vice versa, but as this is brand new technology, there is also a lot of middle ground for both of us to explore.

After a few more meetings and several more coffees at our regular Meeting Room C (For Costa Coffee), we have a couple of ideas that we want to explore together for VR: one from Paul and one from me.

The two things we both realised quickly were that 1) VR can be lonely once you are immersed in your own world. Back then you experienced VR in your own headset and could not share the fun with other people. And 2) The VR experience was very restrictive, since you were limited to the cable length that linked you to your PC and you couldn't really "go" anywhere other than using a controller to move about in the content you saw. However, because a VR experience is incredibly lifelike, moving around using a controller not only breaks the VR immersion, but occasionally makes people experience motion sickness and that is not a nice feeling.

So, both of our ideas have three things in common: they will allow the VR user to experience VR content together with their friends, colleagues or family (multiplayer); they will allow the VR user to go "somewhere" freely and naturally without a controller; and they will allow total VR immersion.

After a number of sketches, plans and lots of ideas jotted here and there on pieces of paper, we finally decide to put it all together in a digital format. We produce two potential products to market plans and create our company together. It's now August 2014, only a few months since we first met and we already have a registered limited company ready to operate, two potential products and a plan of action.

If we had known at the time what a roller coaster the next two and a half years were going to be, would we have done it? If I had been asked that question in early 2017, the answer would have been, "No Way!" But time has passed, and if someone asked me that question now, in 2019, I would definitely say, "Yes – bring it on!" Don't get me wrong, I would definitely not look forward to going through the pain and headaches it brought, but the experiences, knowledge gained and opportunities to work on ground-breaking products were amazing.

We are not wasting time. It's now December 2014, only four months since we created our limited company, and we've received our Oculus DK2 VR headsets. The DK2 is the second iteration of the original Oculus Kickstarter campaign, and is a much improved headset with a 1920x1080-pixel resolution compared to the 1280x800 resolution of the DK1. This is twice the original number of pixels, with the DK2 now able to display over two million pixels. In VR, every additional pixel of resolution means an improved quality of visuals, so the higher the resolution, the better it is!

We have recently been in contact with what we have found to be the only other company in the world at that time that have also been working on the same concept we have. They are based in Redmond near Seattle in the USA.

After several conference calls with the three members of their founding team, we realise that they are nowhere near as advanced as their website makes them out to be.

We have discussed the option to do a deal with them, but, as it would have limited us to be a non-exclusive distributor of their technology for the UK, it did not sound interesting whatsoever for us, so we dropped the idea and continued with our planned concepts.

We would end up meeting the team a year or so later and they would try out our technology and we would end up trying theirs too. As of today, our company no longer exists; theirs has deployed their systems across 15 countries in locations such as casinos, theme parks and arcades and has had two successful rounds of investments in excess of three million dollars each! Interesting how similar paths in life can take us to completely opposite situations!

So, part of our recent work has essentially been to prepare for an initial test to make sure our idea can work. We have made some modifications to the DK2 headset so we can run it with a longer HDMI cable. I have prepared our first VR content – a simple 3D room made to look like an abandoned house with no lights – using the Unity 3D software which was yet to become the mainstream VR development platform it is today. We have been trusted by Vicon Systems – one of the world's largest motion capture system companies – with £20k worth of equipment for two weeks, entirely free of charge, so we can test our concept. I guess they liked our ideas and realised that this could open a brand new market for them, since their equipment is essentially used to produce special effects in Hollywood blockbusters and not for the purpose we are using it.

We've even put together a "Cardboard" VR headset using a Samsung Note and streaming the content from a PC to the phone via the Nvidia streaming engine. The purpose of the "Cardboard VR," launched by Google a few months before, was for everyone to experience VR using their own smartphone as a makeshift VR headset. The idea is good, but it is neither great quality, nor a great experience and does not have any tracking, so it is a rather poor experience for people trying VR for the first time.

You see, one of our goals of being able to go "somewhere" in VR is to have a wireless headset so we are not restricted by cable length. However, this has to be balanced with the other key element we need to achieve for immersive VR, which is to have ultra-realistic graphics with minimum latency and only PCs are able to produce those. This is why we have modified the original idea of the "Cardboard VR" headset to stream the content from a PC instead of using the Samsung Note's processing power.

Streaming content from a PC to a phone has its drawbacks, namely connection issues, but, more importantly, added latency. In brief, latency is the duration it takes from the time you turn your head to the time the graphics on the screen you are looking at have turned the same way. That duration needs to be kept at a bare minimum, otherwise the experience is unrealistic and it introduces motion sickness.

Our plans are to design and develop our very own wireless headset and we have started working on a prototype that we are using to try out several different technologies and technics, but this is nowhere near ready. The two biggest difficulties are to find a suitable wireless channel that can carry over two million pixels every second and to have a lightweight battery pack that can supply a screen and a wireless receiver power requirement long enough without weighing too much.

With various tools, Paul and I have worked out that our initial prototype streaming headset latency is around the 40ms to 50ms (millisecond) mark which, in terms of VR, is a lot. The DK2 – because it is wired – is somewhere around the 20ms mark. As of 2019, modern VR headsets - are below the 10ms mark!

For now, we need to establish how well our optical tracking idea can work, as this is the key element to being able to have multiplayers walking around in VR over a large area. To test if our concept could work, we are going to use our wireless Samsung phone in our cardboard headset as well as a wired DK2 with extended cable length. (It is important to note that this is the end of 2014 and the only wired VR headset available on the market at the moment is the Oculus DK2.)

It has taken us several days to assemble the equipment correctly, but thanks to the assistance of Vicon's engineers, we have managed to set up a multi-camera optical tracking system over an area of 20 square metres (around 220 square foot). We have now attached the tracking markers to our VR headsets (both our Samsung Cardboard and Oculus DK2) and to our flashlight –a real flashlight bought in a hardware store.

We had to develop some custom scripts to collect the tracking data from the Vicon optical tracking system and import them in real time into our Unity 3D designed content.

To clarify the challenge we faced, I will briefly explain what optical tracking is and its purpose. If you are not interested in the technical bits, you can skip the next three paragraphs.

A couple of decades before, as the cinema industry special effects demand increased, a couple of companies started to offer a new technology named motion capture. The concept uses a number of infrared high-resolution cameras placed around a room and focused on the centre of that room where one or more actors play their part. It is often not the principal actor of the movie performing motion capture, rather specially trained people who wear a full-body Lycra suit that has dozens of reflective markers. Those markers are placed strategically on the body to track a body join.

In order for the cameras to accurately track the position of the markers, the room is calibrated in advance using a process that teaches the cameras how far away they are in relation to the centre of the room, as well as where they are in that room. To be tracked, a reflective marker must be visible by at least three cameras at any one time (this is called the triangulation process). If more cameras see the markers, the result is even more accurate. The triangulation process is able to work out where in that room each marker is and the results are transmitted to a computer as an X, Y, Z coordinate, which is a number expressed in distance from the centre of the room as Left position, Forward position and Height.

Vicon then provide a number of options where each marker can be linked with a digital skeleton. The result means that the digital skeleton on the screen moves exactly as the real person in the room does. With special computer animation, it is then easy to attach the skeleton to any type of fictional character and make it appear incredibly lifelike.

However, the way we are planning to use the Vicon system is quite different. We do not want to use a Lycra suit, as this would take too long for the players to get prepared and would be inconvenient as well as requiring a lot of calibration. We want to use the same technology, but attach it to objects instead, such as our VR headset or some props like a weapon or flashlight. To do this, we've prepared our headset and one flashlight with a number of strategically placed markers. We have grouped them as single objects, which means that we now get six coordinates for each. These are their X, Y and Z positions in the room as per before, but also their angular positions, which are known as the Yaw, Pitch and Roll positions. The Yaw is the angle to which the object is rotated right or left on its vertical axis compared to the original – or zero – position; the Pitch is the angle the object is pointing up or down compared to the zero position; and the Roll is the angle that object is banking right or left on its horizontal axis in relation to the zero position.

When we combine those six coordinates, we now have not only the position of the object in the room, but also its angular position on itself which is all we need to accurately represent that object in our 3D content.

To do this, we've written a script to collect these coordinates four times every second and feed them to our Unity 3D designed game content where we have a camera (which shows what the player sees in the headset) and a flashlight (that lights up the dark room).

The coordinates automatically change the position of the camera and the flashlight in the games according to the real movements made on the headset and the flashlight. What we have done is to essentially motion track objects in a game content. This was already doable with the technology Vicon had at the time, but not in real time, only as a recorded track which would not have worked for us.

So, we've set up our first ever test in our local technological hub, Digital Jersey. The venue only opened a couple of years before and provided us a large enough space to assemble our first free roaming VR experience on a weekend when the place was quiet.

Paul is the first to try it, headset on and flashlight in his hand. The Vicon tracking system can see the headset and flashlight and is reproducing every move into our Unity 3D content. This is a single derelict room that I have built using the Unity 3D game engine, with only the light of the thunder outside and riddled with old furniture and junk inside.

The moment of truth . . . a scream of excitement from Paul tells me that it is working. I can see on my monitor what he can see in his headset. He is using his flashlight to look around the room and taking a few steps forward to explore it. He can turn freely around, bend down, crouch and use the flashlight in his hand to light up the virtual room as if it were a real flashlight. Every move of the headset and the flashlight is replicated in the content and sent in near-real time to his headset, giving him the incredible feeling that it is all real.

It is not perfect, far from it. It is a little jittery and, tracking is not entirely accurate and there is some latency, but for a first test it has exceeded our expectations. We are over the moon – we have created what must be one of the first free roam VR systems in the world.

We are not naive enough to think we are the first. We know there are many other people in the world trying to achieve something similar and, over the next few months, we would end up meeting and talking to a few of them. but, for the time being, we feel on top of the world.

MY FAVOURITE QUOTE

"The people who are crazy enough to think they can change the world are the ones who do."
Steve Jobs –Apple founder and CEO

LESSON LEARNED:

I've selected this quote from the great Steve Jobs because this is the way I felt back then. We were working on brand new technology that very few people had tried and we were developing new opportunities.

Having said that, even if they are not going to change the world, when I develop products for clients as a freelance software developer, I always thrive in finding the angle, the opportunity and the difference the product is going to make to everyone using it. This approach can make the difference between a great product and an amazing one!

WHAT WOULD YOU HAVE DONE?

I have decided to do something a little unusual and involve you in this story. To do so, in each of the book's chapters starting from Chapter Two, you will see a choice of possible alternatives to what we did. It is just a little quiz for you to ask how you would have done it if you had been in my / our shoes.

I have set up a website where you can share your choices anonymously if you wish. This is just for fun and you can also see what other people who have read this book and voted think.

So, if you would like to share the way you would have done it, head to **1b1m1y.com**
and click on "I would have done it this way."

CHAPTER TWO

How much investment?

It's been a year since Paul and I first met and, when we look back over the last 12 months, it's quite insane to see how far we have progressed.

It is February 2015. We have managed to get a working wireless headset – albeit still very much a prototype – and we are able to track someone over a 20 square metre (210 square foot) area fairly well, including the use of props.

We have our business logo, brochures, flyers, a live website and we have even started working on our second idea – my personal one – which is to develop a VR motion simulator to replicate the excitement of being in a race car.

What we need now is more money to purchase a full Vicon optical tracking system as well as to transform our headset prototype into something a bit more commercial. We have both invested a fair bit of our own money into this project already, as any company founders do, but we now need to take this further and higher. This opportunity arrives when we are introduced to a lady named Melissa.

Melissa is business minded as well, she likes tech and she is looking to invest some of her money into new opportunities. We show her what we have developed, she tries it and, after a few meetings, we come to an agreement and she offers to invest £30k into our company in return for 20% of shares.

It's not a huge amount of money for the shareholding offered, but we need that money in order to take us to the next level, so we have little choice. However, it ends up being a great decision, as Melissa is not only a source of funds, she is now also involving herself in the company and soon becomes our marketing person with great results.

We have spent the £30k very wisely. We have purchased our own optical tracking system with eight tracking cameras that allow us to track up to four people and four props in VR in an area of up to 60 square metres (645 square foot). It is, however, only accurate for about two thirds of that area, as the corners of the zone are not well covered by the tracking system.

We have also purchased new computer equipment for better VR, an additional two Oculus DK2, and we also have our first wireless VR headset. Now, when I say wireless, it is without any wires (of course), but it is not perfect – far from it. The technology we are using is running on the 60GHz frequency and presents a number of challenges, such as requiring a line of sight between the transmitter and receiver on the headset as well as being incredibly sensitive to interferences like mobile phones, magnets and so on.

As a safety net, we have three headsets: our main prototype wireless headset running on the 60Ghz band; (see photo, page 163) our backup headset which is our first concept using a Galaxy Note and streaming content to it from the PC; and, finally, an extended Oculus DK2 (however, this having a cable is not ideal when people are going to be walking around a reasonably large area.)

We also have two racing simulation seats with advanced controllers, which are configured to run a popular racing game, together with an Oculus DK2. There was very little creation from us for these two simulators other than putting different bits together, but the purpose was to better understand the requirements and to get people's feedback to help us build the next generation of driving simulators which is what my idea is all about.

26th June 2015. This is the official launch day of Vizuality Studios! We have been in the local and national press for a few weeks now. We have invited several hundred people from various industries (education, architecture and tech) and we are launching at the Jersey's grand Radisson Blu Hotel on the Waterfront.

We have a large stage set up, so we have invited several industry speakers, and, in the room, we have our 60 square metre VR setup and two simulators. Over the day, hundreds of people will be testing out our setup while we make note of their comments and feedback.

The launch was a success. We've had excellent feedback and we know we are on the right track now, so, following the launch, we start to look for a permanent base for our new VR studio.

We can see great potential for our technology in gaming, but, more importantly, we think there is huge potential to use VR for architectural representation as well as for the entertainment industry, like cinemas, and we want to be ready early. We have set our sights on an old nightclub that was left abandoned a few years ago. It requires a lot of work, but the space is amazing and the location is ideal to provide every type of VR we want.

We have visited our "future studio" several times, and have started to get some architectural designs for the interior modifications. We are getting quotes for the various refurbishments needed and are in the process of negotiating a lease with the landlord.

The three months that followed our official launch were very busy. Aside from the ongoing developments and improvement on our tracking and wireless headset, we were solicited for a number of events, applied for a local government business funding scheme and had three meetings with potential investors.

One of those investment meetings came very close to being accepted; however, we eventually felt that the £100k financial offer was not sufficient for the 30% shareholding requested (another decision that we would look back on at a later stage wondering, "What if we had accepted that offer?" as it came from a very successful businessman!)

It is the middle of September 2015. Our official launch was only two and half months ago, but it already feels an eternity away because so much has happened since then. Paul, being a network and PC hardware technician during his day job, has been doing some work on James' home computer. James and Paul both have their children in the same school and got to know each other that way.

During one of his home visits to James, Paul tells him what we do and how our technology is pushing boundaries in the world of VR. James is not a technical guy by any means, but his background and experience was to be the unusual chance meeting that we needed back then.

A few days later, James mentions to Paul that he really would like to see our setup and to see what we do, as he may be interested in investing in us. Paul mentions this to me and, since we have another event at the Radisson Hotel again the following week, we happily oblige and invite James to come and have a look.

In the last few weeks, in order to showcase what we do to as many people as possible, we have been setting up our motion VR studio for a number of free events and we are lined up for a few more over the coming two months. We have even booked ourselves into the Technology Expo which is due to be held on the 5th and 6th of October 2015 at the Vinopolis in London. The exhibition is free to attend, so we just have to ship our kit across and be there for a few days. The exhibition is coined as, "The very first VR and AR-orientated exhibition," so we cannot miss that. The only small issue is that this is a table-style exhibition where exhibitors are given a booth space around three metres long with a table and chair to discuss their tech with visitors. After several discussions with the organisers, however, we have managed to get the end side of the second exhibition hall with over 40 square metres (430 square foot) to ourselves, so we're going to be the biggest display there!

James arrives for the demonstration as planned, along with a lady who he introduces to us as a work colleague, but is in fact one of our future investors. This visit is followed by a couple of meetings where we discuss our background, the technology and ideas and our future plans and then, only a couple of weeks after we first introduced our business to James, he make us an offer of investment . . . and what an offer!

The broad term of the offer is £1,670,000 (that's 1.6million pounds or 2.1million dollars) provided by four HNWI (High Net Worth Individuals) and backed by an initial 12-month handwritten forecast that details the investment funding in several instalments.

Broadly, this is to be split into a £420,000 initial investment followed by three lump payments of £170k each in March, May and July 2016 and then two final payments of £370k each in September and November 2016. Half of the money is an investment; the second half is to be an unsecured business loan that the company will have to repay in three years' time with only interest to pay in the meantime. The first payment is to include a £50k sum to buy out Melissa's shares, leaving Paul and I with 22% each. It is more than we would like to give at this stage in shareholding percentage, but, in another way, it is best to have a small percentage of something big than a big percentage of something small!

James is an investment broker and invests money from some of his wealthy contacts into businesses and placements for higher returns, so we feel that this is the right way for our company to go.

I have to pinch myself – surely this is too good to be true? There are so many start-ups that look for funding for ages and even when those start-ups find investments, it is often a few hundred thousand pounds at most. We, within a couple of months of our launch, with a product that is not even good enough commercially yet, get an offer of £835k investment backed by an £835k unsecured business loan. Yes, of course, half of that money will be on the basis of a repayable loan from the company to the investors, but the terms are incredibly good and we have three years to pay it back. We've discussed and agreed with Paul that, "If we haven't managed to make that much profit within the next three years then there will likely be no company left by then anyway," and this is exactly what our company needs to take it to the big stage.

The following few weeks are totally manic. Due diligence, investor background checks, lawyers, shareholding agreements to review and sign, meetings after meetings, discussions with Melissa about her exit, and finally the day arrives!

31st October 2015. Melissa has accepted a generous exit deal to buy back her shares.

James has become a 2% shareholder, and the four investors have become 54% shareholders between them. We are now officially a "big" company with seven shareholders in total and a board of directors with three executive directors. James becomes the chairman and financial director; Paul is co-CEO and technical director; and I am co-CEO and lead developer.

MY FAVOURITE QUOTE

"When I'm old and dying, I plan to look back on my life and say, 'Wow, that was an adventure,' not, 'Wow, I sure felt safe. "
Tom Preston-Werner – co-founder of GitHub

LESSON LEARNED:

I've chosen that quote as it is so relevant in so many ways to me in this chapter. I'm not a gambler in life, I don't even play the National Lottery! As far as business is concerned, I have taken risks in the past, but as long as I have carefully assessed that these risks are minimal and the chances of success are high, I will take them.

I had been a small business owner for over 14 years before that day. I had even set up a business and sold it for a six-figure sum three years before then, but I still viewed myself as a halfway entrepreneur where I have the will, skills and ideas to develop new tech and challenge known concepts, but, on the other hand, I am most likely too cautious when it comes to investing large sums of money into anything new.

So, while I knew we had a product that was very unique and while we were at the dawn of the VR revolution – which made me confident that we should be able to succeed – this offer of investment was just incomprehensible at first! It's not that I did not believe it was true, as James came with serious credentials and the investors he proposed to bring in were well established business people, but it was such a huge amount of money for a young company to receive that it just did not seem possible at first.

There were a lot of questions in my head: "Why so much money? What do we need all this money for? Do we really need that much? Are we giving too much equity away?" Being director and CEO of a big company and being responsible for this huge funding was a scary prospect, and it was equally scary to suddenly become a bigger company with a board of directors, shareholders and multiple employees as well as having to sign complex, lawyer-written agreements that only made sense to lawyers. At the same time, though, I knew this was the opportunity of a lifetime and would unlikely happen again. Hence the selected quote!

WHAT WOULD YOU HAVE DONE?

As per my introduction in the first chapter, here is your chance to start sharing your views and feedback on what you would have done had you been in my shoes.

1. Would you have stayed with the initial investment of £30k we received and grown the company organically?

2. Would you have accepted the £100k investment for 30% shareholding from the successful businessman?

3. Would you have accepted the same offer as we did for the same shareholding as we did?

Or maybe you would have done it completely differently? If so, please share what you would have done online at **1b1m1y.com**

You can also log in to that website to view what other people would have done.

CHAPTER THREE

Nepotism isn't good

It's early November 2015. It is weird to look back as I write this book to think that within the next 12 months, it would be nearly all over for us. It is also frustrating to look back on some of the companies we met during that time and classified as competitors to see that they are doing rather well these days!

Today, we have set up at a regional event. It is a family-themed agricultural event, so not exactly the type suited for our technology. However, as we are keen to showcase what we do to as many people as possible, we have accepted nearly every invite we have received in recent weeks so we are now getting rather good at setting up our VR studio. The full setup "only" takes us a couple of hours now! The technology is working OK and we are delighted to showcase our product to people while working to improve and develop it further.

As the investment offer has now been finalised and the first lump payment of £440k has been credited to our business account, James is visiting us at the event and he has come with a friend named Stan who he introduces to us as a potential salesperson for our growing company.

Stan is a confident guy; he has the salesman chat but he reeks of alcohol! OK, sure, this is the weekend and he is off duty so everyone is free to do whatever they want in their own time, but if you are going to come and meet your potential employers, even casually and recommended by your friend James, surely you make an effort, no?

He tells Paul and I that he is this ace car salesman, but not just any cars – he is the top performing salesman for the likes of Aston Martins.

Obviously, this event is not the ideal place to discuss this as we are always busy with people wanting to have a go and adjusting the system and fixing the small bugs that happen in such a new offering. Once the event is finished, Paul and I have a discussion about this, and two things come out of it. One is that the first impression wasn't great, and the second is, "Do we need a salesperson right now when we have not got a product fully ready yet?"

It is a mixed feeling. Yes, a salesperson is crucial to any business, but is it the right time? We feel that we are still a good six months away from having a commercially ready-to-sell product, so we're not sure. Anyway, James is adamant that the company needs a salesperson sooner rather than later; that having the opportunity to have someone like Stan on board would not be happening again; and even if we don't have a product ready, we need to start marketing it and the company immediately. Lo and behold . . . the next thing we know, Stan will be starting with us on the 15th of December!

"Paul, did we agree to that or did we get convinced to agree?" I ask. I'm not sure what happened there really! Anyway, we now have a "Head of Worldwide Sales!"

Impressive title, isn't it? Not sure who decided it, but that is what Stan's job title is! Surely with a title like that, the sales are going to be rolling in. . .

The plan for our studio in the old nightclub has fallen through, as another local business has made a bid for the lease. This is not actually such bad news, as we have got our eyes set on a new location just outside town, which is an old TV studio and has a massive single room that would make a perfect VR studio.

It is early December now. The last four weeks have been totally manic, things are happening faster than I can keep up with and Paul and I have now started our very long work pattern of around 16 hours a day on average that would become the norm for the next 12 months.

We've ordered our first motion simulator platform to go with our VR simulator development.

Stan will be our second employee as Mikey – a young motorsports university graduate – has also just started with us to be our simulator programmer and work on the VR simulator with me.

We're meeting with a local marketing company to redesign our company identity, our brochures, business card and website. Paul and I are a little reluctant about some of the work proposed as it is rather expensive. They have quoted us £10k for the website redesign, £16k for our full rebranding, including the printing of brochures and business cards, and a further £10k on a promotional video. That's nearly £50,000 to spend, and we can do a lot of this inhouse. I have built plenty of websites and have done some video editing work in the past as well, so we could do some of it ourselves.

However, James is reassuring us that this is the right thing to do. Paul and I are too busy with development work on our prototypes and new products and our time is better spent on this than doing a website that other people can do for us. I guess James is right – and we go for it.

We have also just spent around £75,000 purchasing new computer equipment, additional tracking cameras and more components for our headsets. Have we really just spent over £120k in the last couple of weeks? I guess it's worth it – this is all hardware and components required to make our product commercially finished and to complete the development of our second offering.

It is scary to see how quickly the budget can be spent, but it was discussed at our board meetings and jointly decided between all directors that this was the right way for the company to go, so all is good.

James is busy getting some architectural plans and technical drawings for our new studio. As per the previous location, this one will require a lot of work, but once completed, it should be amazing, have huge opportunity for expansion and give us a very solid base.

MY FAVOURITE QUOTE

"In America, we have anti-nepotism laws in the federal government and in lots of state governments, because the practice of hiring relatives undermines public confidence that the government official is actually finding the best person for the job."
Kathleen Clark –American playwright

LESSON LEARNED:

I've selected Ms Clark's quote because, in our case, it could not be any more relevant. You will discover this over the next few chapters due to the various events that happened because of the relationship between Stan and James.

My lesson here is that first impressions count. Trust your gut feelings; if it doesn't feel right, then it probably isn't. – This should serve as a reminder to me, because I already knew that.

I'm not sure whether I was persuaded into accepting Stan on board or whether I had not been strong enough to stand up and say no.

WHAT WOULD YOU HAVE DONE?

1. Would you have waited another six months at least before recruiting any salespeople?

2. Would you have recruited a salesperson now, but definitely not a friend of James?

3. Would you have done what we did (or what we were persuaded to do) and dealt with whatever challenges came with it?

Or maybe you would have done it completely differently? If so, please share what you would have done online at **1b1m1y.com**

You can also log in to that website to view what other people would have done.

CHAPTER FOUR

First of many opportunities

Despite having spent nearly a quarter of our initial investment already, our company bank account has a large positive balance. It's the middle of December 2015 and, during an extensive board of directors meeting, we are discussing what the company needs to do in 2016 to make the most of our investment.

We are sharing ideas and plans on what the company should allocate its budget for during the coming year. With the specialised press now talking a lot about VR and announcing that 2016 is going to be "The year of VR", James wants us to attend VR events in the USA. "If we are going to break into this industry, we have to be where it all happens. We have to be in Silicon Valley!"

says James. "We have to showcase what we do quickly and to the right people in order to be noticed and be able to raise more funding," James adds.

Paul and I are stunned. We've just received our initial seed funding and James is already talking of further investments!

This is a little beyond me, but, admittedly, I like the idea of sharing what we do with more people which is what we have been doing for the last few months. If we can now do that at the centre of the tech world – Silicon Valley itself -– where all the other VR newcomers are, then that sounds exciting and the right thing to do. Paul, however, is more reserved and would prefer to hold off a little longer. He is not entirely against it, but he is more cautious.

This is one of our very first board meetings, we are three directors and we have three separate views on this. Paul isn't especially in agreement on attending the shows, essentially due to the huge logistic costs involved, but also believes that we should continue to work on the product and make it better before showcasing it. While I agree with Paul, I still think we should attend them as we need to keep our finger on the pulse and see what is being done in our industry and what competitors are doing. I think that only Paul and I should travel (essentially because we know the product and the industry well by now), maybe with a small booth showcasing our work eventually. James, however, thinks we should go big. "Let's go and show them who we are, let's get people to try our tech, let's show investment companies that we are here and we mean business," were his convincing phrases! So, we were three directors with three clearly different ideas from one extreme to the other. Not a great start!

The decision is made: our first ever international event is going to be the Vision Summit, held in Los Angeles in the middle of February 2016.

Why the Vision Summit? Well, Unity 3D – the development platform for VR – is presenting the event, as they are placing their product as the leading development tool for VR content.

There are also going to be a number of newcomers: Microsoft are bringing their HoloLens to a selected pre-booked audience; HTC Vive are launching their new headset; Oculus will be showcasing their upcoming CV1 headset due to be launched in March 2016; and a fair few new VR companies will be there. There will also be lots of press people too, so this is a great opportunity.

Since there isn't too much work for Stan to do at this moment, James gets him to organise the trip. Five of us are flying business class to Los Angeles. We are going to stay at the Loews Hotel in the middle of Hollywood – oh, and we will be sponsoring the event as well! Ouch! That is nearly £30k spent on one event. Paul isn't happy, "Do we need to fly business class? Do we have to stay at that expensive hotel? What is the point of sponsoring the event?"

Aside from the Vision Summit event, we are also looking at attending the VRX Europe in London, SVVR in San Jose, Laval Virtual in France and a few more events during the upcoming year.

A few of them are quickly confirmed for March and April 2016, so it looks like it is going to be a busy three months from February onwards. Is this wise? Should we not spend more time finishing the development of our headset – still at prototype status – as well as our simulator which only exists on paper at the moment?

It is at another one of our board meetings that we all agree to go with James' view. He has convincing arguments, I guess, and two of the recent companies he brokered investments for have had good success. More importantly, he has been explaining the essentials of investments to us, based on his years as an investment broker. He says that to become a top world player in business, we have to grab the attention of the big investors, and we are only going to do this if we show how different we are and how serious we are about it.

It is also at about this time that we sign our first partnership agreement with a UK / USA-based furniture design company. They have many contracts with a large number of retailers, including very well known names like IKEA and Wren, and they think our technology could be used in stores to showcase new room designs to customers. We also sign a separate agreement with a software development company that has an interior design solution that has been on the market for over 20 years. They, too, see the potential of free roam VR as a means to sell furniture to customers. They have a team of 20 salespeople all over the UK and thousands of clients. These are very exciting opportunities for us.

Also around this time, we start to plan to add a third product to be developed over the coming year. We are discussing the concept with a local engineer about what we are aiming to achieve. In brief, the idea is to develop an improved motion simulator allowing a full 360-degrees motion in VR to be able to eventually simulate flying aircraft or spaceships.

MY FAVOURITE QUOTE

"I owe my success to having listened respectfully to the very best advice, and then going away and doing the exact opposite."
Gilbert K Chesterton – English writer, poet and philosopher

LESSON LEARNED:

I've selected this quote from Mr Chesterton as maybe this is what we should have done with James' advice. You see, when someone backs their decision with sound experience in a domain that you are a total newbie in (financial investment and growing of companies in this instance for me and Paul), it is unprofessional to not listen to it, but also difficult to stand your ground and say, "No, we respect your advice but we still think it is best to do it our way."

Having said that, I am going to contradict myself a little, as it may not have been the wrong decision. As you will read in the upcoming chapters, going out with our guns blazing brought a number of incredible opportunities. Would we have managed to get those opportunities if it had not been for that assertive approach?

WHAT WOULD YOU HAVE DONE?

1. Would you have been more like Paul and waited to attend any events and carried on working on the products to develop them further?

2. Would you have been more like me and attended some events, but with a small booth and only a couple of us to keep an eye on the trends and competition?

3. Would you have done what James suggested, and what we eventually did, and go full guns blazing?

Or maybe you would have done it completely differently? If so, please share what you would have done online at **1b1m1y.com**

You can also log in to that website to view what other people would have done.

CHAPTER FIVE

The year of VR

It's January 2016, the dawn of the Year of VR everybody is talking about. This year is going to be the big one for VR, and we feel that we are going to play a major part in that revolution. As such, James thinks that we need to restructure the business. We have several meetings with our new accountant and a new proposed structure is put in place.

James has decided that we should change our accountant to someone who will be able to handle our growing company better. The previous accountant that Paul and I had for the last 18 months did a good job and, considering that the company has had very little revenue so far, has been charging very little. As such, we are not especially keen to change, but James is insisting that this new accountant is what our company needs.

So, we have now moved to this new accountant who will be handling our business restructuring, changing from a single limited company to five distinct limited companies.
There is Vizuality Ltd, Vizuality Studios Ltd, Vizuality Designs Ltd and Vizuality Services Ltd as well as a fifth company named Augmented Illusions Ltd, which is essentially the name of the first company we created before opening Vizuality Studio and is now a dormant company.

Under this new structure, we are all shareholders of the five companies as well as directors. There is also a pool of B shares that has been created and we all get allocated a number of them while some are reserved for the first few staff members. It is my understanding that those shares will become very valuable as the companies increase in value and essentially represent a potential high value in the future that we can sell if we want.

One of the requirements that comes from James and the shareholders is that I wind down my existing freelance software development company. Up until now, Paul and I have continued to work within our respective businesses, but now James explains that the shareholders expect our full commitment to this company.

This is fully understandable, but I explain to them that this is not really possible as I have clients that pay me regular fees to maintain their websites, apps and other products I have developed for them. I cannot let them down and, while I fully understand that they want my full commitment to this new company, I can only agree that I will complete the app project I currently have in development and will not take on any more development work.

We come to an agreement on that basis and decide that within 12 months I will need to sell the company or hand over my clients to a different organisation so that my focus is fully on this current company.

After a few more meetings with our new accountant and our lawyer to establish the whole structure, it is all in place. The benefit, I'm told, is that we now have separate companies to hold separate functions. Vizuality Limited is the main company that has received the investment. Vizuality Design Ltd will be holding all of our intellectual properties such as business name and logo registrations, patent applications, trademarks, copyrights and anything else of intellectual value. Vizuality Studios Ltd is where our sales from the various studios we are planning to open and our planned franchising incomes are going to be paid into, while Vizuality Services Ltd will be the company that purchases our company's assets, issues products and services sales invoices, as well as settling the direct suppliers and paying the staff and directors' salaries. Finally, Augmented Illusions Ltd, which was the first name we opened our company under, will remain dormant.

It's strange, but even after having the purpose of the companies explained to me, and having been told that it is standard procedure for larger corporations, I still don't quite understand the purpose or benefits of splitting this into separate companies. At the end of the day, if James, our financial director and chairman, our new accountant and our lawyer are advising this to be the best way forward, then who am I to query it? I've got too much going on with developments of our products anyway!

There will be a sixth limited company set up at a later stage as well, but more on this in a few chapters.

For now, we have received an initial invoice of nearly £5,000 for the setup of these companies.

This comes to me and Paul as a little electric shock. We previously set up our limited company ourselves and it had cost us a couple of hundred pounds. For the overseeing of our company's financial and legal responsibilities, our previous accountant has cost us £800 over the last 18 months. However, this was only the beginning of a much longer list of costs and, overall, during 2016, the various accounting fees and other services rendered – such as company secretary, issues of new shares, valuation, bookkeeping and so on – will end up costing the company £37,000, which I believe could have been avoided or minimised initially while the company was at the early stages of growth.

What we did not know at the time is that this complex company structure was going to come back to seriously bite us later on. More on this towards the end of this book.

Back at the tech expo at the Vinopolis in London a couple of months ago, we met with Jimmy and Mark, the management team of a development studio based in Liverpool. They are doing a lot of VR and AR development and they love what we do and can equally see the huge potential our technology has. Reciprocally, they have a big development team with talented guys who have developed some cool concepts, so there seems to be a natural synergy between us.

We have remained in regular contact with them since, and we keep discussing both our progress and theirs. As such, James, Paul and I have now been back and forth to Liverpool a couple of times to discuss opportunities as well as to brief their development team on helping me to establish our new F1 simulator content.

I initially started with the official Abu Dhabi F1 racetrack – using the Unity 3D engine which I am now getting used to. I have done all of the trackside components and some of the props (trees, emergency vehicles, harbour boats) but, considering how busy our next three months are going to be, I now need help with the development of the pit buildings, grandstands and the various other dynamic elements needed to make the track realistic.

During one of our visits to the Liverpool team, they tell us that they have a number of clients that would be interested in using our studio and they could build custom content for it. James is keen for us to open our first studio in the UK as soon as possible, and the Liverpool team informs us that there is a huge office refurbishment going on right next to their offices. If we are interested in having a look, they can put us in touch with the contractor.

A few days later, another visit to Liverpool is organised following an initial discussion with the contractor in charge of the refurbishment for the three of us to go and have a look at the available space.

Hard hat and high-vis jacket on, we are kindly shown around the various spaces available by the project manager. Paul and I are not very keen on the chosen building. We do like the idea of opening a UK-based studio, and being next door to a successful company would be beneficial, but the building is quite old and does not lend itself to a good large room for a big studio. It is very long, with the floor space nearly 25 metres long, but it is only six metres wide. Additionally, the entrance does not have main street access, so it is not the easiest place to come by unless you know where to find it. It is also a very old building that is difficult to picture as a suitably modern VR studio (See photos, page 164)!

MY FAVOURITE QUOTE

"Don't play games that you don't understand, even if you see lots of other people making money from them."
Tony Hsieh – CEO of Zappos

LESSON LEARNED:

I chose this quote because, in some ways, this is relevant to what happened to us there. "Having a complex structure is normal for larger corporations," we were told, but – hey – we're not a large corporation yet. We've not even got a commercially ready product to sell.

Did we put the horse before the cart? Should we not be concentrating on building up the business first, finishing our products and making some sales before we spend all of this money on accountants and lawyers? Anyway, that is something I will never know since we never had a chance to cash in the B shares or even see how big our corporation structure could grow.

WHAT WOULD YOU HAVE DONE?

1. Would you have stayed as a single limited company at all times, even if the business had grown successfully into a multi-million-pound business?

2. Would you have stayed a single limited company for the time being and then changed to a similar structure at a later stage when the sales were in?

3. Would you agree that this was the right move to do at that time in planning for a big future for the company, taking into consideration the costs to set it up?

Or maybe you would have done it completely differently? If so, please share what you would have done online at **1b1m1y.com**

You can also log in to that website to view what other people would have done.

CHAPTER SIX

The second missed opportunity

It's nearly the end of January 2016. We're only a couple of weeks away from our trip to Los Angeles and our first international event. It's so exciting, but scary at the same time. We're due to meet the representatives of Marvel Studios while at the show. They are coming to see what we are doing and whether it can be used in some promotional events. We have been given Mr Tony Stark's garage in 3D Unity content (that's Iron Man for those of you who wonder who Tony Stark is!) to load on our platform. We can walk around it with our wireless VR headset, have a look out of the windows, walk next to his various tools and Iron Man suits in their glass cabinets, as well as sitting down at Tony's computer workstations. The content is designed in super high resolution, down to the smallest detail with animated robot arms and computer screen displays. It's simply fabulous and being able to use our technology to freely walk around that large VR garage is very exciting.

Our second VR headset, designed for our VR simulator, is taking shape. It is, of course, still a very early prototype built in house, but it works nicely.

It's a high-resolution virtual reality headset built inside a racing helmet. And when I say high-resolution, I mean high resolution! It is using a 2560x1440-pixel resolution on a six-inch screen when, at the time, the Oculus Rift DK2 is using a 1920x1080-pixel resolution. That VR helmet is stunning: it has a built-in fan for anti-mist and to cool the user; it has built-in surround sound; and a built-in bass booster that provides a vibration effect, as well as two-way radio communication.

To make sure it is not affected by the motion of the simulator, we are not using an IMU (Inertial Motion Unit) which is the traditional way of tracking VR headset movements. Instead, the tracking of the head is done externally using carefully placed markers on the helmet together with an externally mounted three-camera optical tracking system.

We have also purchased a replica of half a Formula 1 chassis. The aim is to mount this on our motion platform and provide the ultimate F1 experience: not just a game, but a true total experience with simulated g-force.

Our motion simulator arrived last week, and we've been busy attaching the F1 replica to the simulator, setting it up and configuring it, as James wants us to take it to our first event in the US.

I have connected it to our Unity 3D F1 content, while Mikey is working out the centre of gravity and various balances and weight to ratio stuff in order to adjust the simulator inputs. The first few tests are "interesting," as we can actually sit in the F1 replica, race around our relatively raw F1 track content in our new VR helmet and have our head tracked independently of the simulator's movements.

I say "interesting," as it reminds me of the first test Paul and I did on our motion tracked wireless headset just over a year before. It is exciting to be testing out something that has not been done before – and testing out something that I originally drew on a piece of paper about two years ago – but, equally, this is still very basic. The motion is not perfectly synced with the graphics, so, while I do not suffer from motion sickness, I can see that this is going to affect a number of people. We have a lot of work to do to get this to a more commercial stage, but, like we did with our other headset, we are going to work on this and get it right.

Based on our recent tests and feedback from the simulator, I have advised James that we are unlikely to be able to demonstrate it working properly. Even working flat out for the next couple of weeks will not be enough to have something that is much improved on the current raw display and motion – especially as it needs to be shipped very shortly in order to arrive on time.

However, James is adamant that we must take it with us and showcase what we are working on. We need to show the world what we can do, even if it's not great. We can tell people who try it that this is a prototype and warn them that it is not a finished product.

I must admit that it looks good (see photos, page 165) and I would be very proud to showcase what we are working on, so I am easily convinced to go along and take it with us. Paul is more reserved on the subject and does not think we need to take it, especially as it is going to cost a lot to ship. Paul could be right – are we jumping the gun again? Or, maybe – as per James' decision to want to do these big events, sponsor them and be seen – did this help us in receiving the large number of opportunities that I will describe in the coming chapters?

Would we have had those opportunities if we had not been at the show or if we had been there, but only with a small booth? Who knows?

Talking of opportunities, there is another one that has just landed on our doorstep this month – and it's not a small one! We've been invited to meet with a financial training company about developing a custom multiuser VR training platform to train workers in the finance industry to spot people's unusual behaviour.

The idea is that the trainee will be at a desk in a real-life scenario and people from all walks of life come to the desk to either open an account or perform a transaction. However, unusual behaviours will be hidden in the content that lead to the person either trying to deposit illegal money or providing fake documentation and so on. After a few meetings, the plan is to form a new joint 50 / 50 company where we will provide the equipment and content and the training company will place the product with their clients. It's a win-win situation.

I've designed a replica of a well-known bank, complete with characters and a couple of initial scenarios in my usual Unity 3D platform. It is usable, can be demonstrated and it looks pretty cool. Unfortunately on this occasion, I'm not entirely sure what happened, but nothing came out of this opportunity. There has never been proper feedback given and, considering that we were so busy for the next few months, none of us really took the time to handle this and it became a missed opportunity without ever knowing where it went wrong. Such a shame, really.

Our motion simulator and replica F1 chassis are packed; all our truss equipment as well as computers, cameras and the various props required are packed; and everything is ready to be shipped to the US for our first event.

We have three huge crates weighing a total of 1.6 tons. To put things in perspective, that's the weight of two small cars of equipment in transit.

Thankfully, the shipping company we are using is amazing; they have already organised the US pre-entry forms and all the handling on both sides of the pond. It will take less than a week to get there and will be delivered to us a couple of days before the event, picked up again afterwards and shipped back to us. The total cost of the transit is over £8,000. That's a lot of money for one event, but I guess it is not that expensive when we consider the huge amount of items to move (see photos, page 162).

The next time we'll see those crates will be at the Loews Hotel in Hollywood . . .

MY FAVOURITE QUOTE

"If you really want to do something, you'll find a way. If you don't, you'll find an excuse."
Jim Rohn – American entrepreneur, author and motivational speaker

LESSON LEARNED:

I absolutely love that quote. Let me ask you, "How many times in your life have you heard people giving you excuses for this or that not being done or for this project not being achievable?"

On this occasion, getting ready for the first event was without a doubt one of the biggest challenges I had to work on in my life up to that point. For the eight weeks between the decision being made to attend the event and the actual event taking place, we had been working pretty much non-stop. No Christmas break for me or Paul and around 16 hours a day is about right – but it was worth every minute of it.

At the end of the day, we have a group of people that have trusted us with their money – and quite a lot of it as well – so we can't let them down.

We only have one go at this and we have to absolutely give it our best shot. There is no way I am turning up in Los Angeles not ready for our first international event regardless of what it takes.

WHAT WOULD YOU HAVE DONE?

1. Would you have made the decision not to take the simulator to the event, saving lots of money in shipping costs but also reducing pressure to have something ready on time?

2. Would you have made the decision to take the simulator, but maybe only part of it like the chassis only and showcase it as a static product of what is to come?

3. Would you have done what we did and taken the entire setup, even knowing full well in advance that it was not going to work properly?

Or maybe you would have done it completely differently? If so, please share what you would have done online at **1b1m1y.com**

You can also log in to that website to view what other people would have done.

CHAPTER SEVEN

Ego trip

It's the 6th of February 2016. We've arrived at Heathrow Airport Terminal 5. There are five of us: me, James, Stan, Paul and Mikey. We're staying at the Sofitel in five rooms booked for the night as our flight to LA is the next morning. Yes – the Sofitel is conveniently located within the airport terminal, but is it wise to stay here when we're at a stage where we're not even making our own money yet as a business? That's over £2,500 of hotel bills if we include dinner and drinks for one single night!

We're travelling with all our prototype headsets and we've also got a couple of suitcases filled with Dremel, glue guns, spare cables, electronic components and spare parts.

Also in our suitcases, we've got our new company suits: smart beige trousers and a blue jacket from Hackett London as well as a white shirt and customised cufflinks. James came back from London a few weeks ago with them; the total cost of the suits and cufflinks was £4,000.

This was one of the first disagreements we had as directors. We discussed the need to have a company identify uniform at one of our board meetings. Paul and I were keen to get a new set of short-sleeved shirts with our logo on it, like we had with our previous logo, which we would then wear with black trousers. However, James said that we needed to have a proper suit in order to show a unified brand. We did raise the concern that because our event was in California, it was going to be hot and suits may not be the right uniform. Anyway, James won this dispute and told us that he would sort it out. We obviously did not expect at the time that he would come back with a branded expensive single suit and cufflinks that did not even have our company logo on them! I still recall Paul's face when I told him the cost – he was as stunned as me!

James also has our new US Dollar company card. He advised a week or so ago that it would be more cost-effective for us to get a credit card in dollars with £5,000 deposited on it so we could pay the hotel balance, meals and other small purchases while in the US. This was to avoid paying conversion charges on every transaction. Paul and I agreed this was a good idea (or maybe it wasn't – as you'll read later!)

It's the morning of our flight to LA. It is scheduled to take off at lunchtime and will last around 11 hours, so after a breakfast at the Sofitel, we are now splitting up. Half the team is flying with Virgin Atlantic and the other half on British Airways.

This is only because James is not a comfortable flyer and suggested that, as a safety measure since Paul and I are the "brains" of the business, we should fly in a separate airline in case one of them crash!

So, while Paul and Mikey head to Terminal 3 to take their Virgin Atlantic flight, James, Stan and I go on to British Airways. A quick check-in process and security, and we are now at the Terminal 5 Business Lounge. After a couple of hours' wait, it is time to board our plane and, as we do so, for the first time in my life I "turn left" to business class. I'm not used to travelling this way. It is, of course, very nice, and for a short stay trip like this one where we will not only be busy but also have to be in full action right away, it does make sense to ensure we arrive fresh and don't suffer as much from jet lag. However, I'm still reserved on the cost of it considering it's still very early days of the company. We could have gone a few days earlier in standard class and saved a fair amount of money.

It's 5pm local time and we've just landed in Los Angeles. After clearing US customs and collecting our bags, we exit onto the Tom Bradley International Terminal. There is a seven-hour time difference between Los Angeles and the UK, so it is good that we've managed to get some sleep on the flight over as, for our body clocks, it is around 1am. We are now waiting for our transfer to the hotel that James booked before leaving.

"Oh, there it is!" says James. I look in the direction he is pointing and see this huge Hummer Limo coming towards us.

"What is that?" I say. I mean, a Hummer is a pretty big car as it is, so you really can't miss a Hummer Limo!

"It's our transfer to the hotel," says James.

"What – for the three of us?!"

"Well, yes it will have to be. I thought we could all go back in it, but didn't account for the difference in our flight arrival times."

You see, since Paul and Mikey are flying with a different airline, they will be arriving at Terminal 2 a couple of hours after us. We are also due to meet up with Jimmy and Mark, our colleagues from Liverpool who are also joining us for the event, but they too will be arriving on a different flight a few hours later, having flown directly from Manchester.

So here we are on our way back to the hotel – the three of us in this party Hummer Limo. James is sitting on one side, I'm in the middle and Stan is on the other end; there must be about five metres between us! Meanwhile, another transfer has to be booked for the other two parts of the team. The cost of the operation is around $400 in total: a pretty expensive transfer if you ask me! Why did we need to turn up in this Limo? This is so poncey!

Anyway, a few hours later the whole team is reunited at the hotel's bar. This is a very nice hotel but, again, I'm not sure it is necessary to stay in such expensive accommodation. Seven rooms booked for six nights there end up costing our company the best part of £10k! I guess the real benefit is that we are at the convention hotel, so we are on site! After a few drinks together, considering it is now nearly 6am UK time and our body clocks are completely upside down, we all head to bed.

Next morning is all hands on deck: our 1.6 tons of equipment has just arrived in the delivery bay of the hotel, two floors below the convention hall. We now have to move everything piece by piece to the location of our booth as the crates obviously do not go in the lift. Let me tell you – it was a very interesting time trying to move our 600kg motion simulator into place. Anyway, by mid-afternoon we're ready to start setting up. We have a bit of time as the conference is not opening until the day after next, so we have the rest of the day and tomorrow to set up and configure our booth. However, considering that this is the first time we are setting up the simulator as well as our full booth, there is quite a bit of guesswork.

That evening, we finish at 2am. I say "we," but I should really say "me and Paul," as the rest of the team left us to finish off by ourselves a long time ago. We didn't really take notice initially, but this was to become a recurring habit at all our subsequent events!

As we complete a very busy day, delighted that we now have our simulator, truss system and cameras all wired and in place with just the calibration and setting up of the content to do the next day, Paul and I decide to stop by the bar for a refreshing drink before going to bed. Lo and behold, we bump into Stan and James in a "party mood," helped by a fair few beverages! That's all we need to "cheer us up" after this hard day's work.

The next day, we resume work on our booth to make sure everything is working well. There are a few issues with our prototype headset's connection and interferences, but it is not bad at all and, overall, I'm happy to show it off to people. After all, we are now exhibiting at one of the very first big VR / AR events with one of the very first PC-driven wireless VR headsets that allows visitors to walk around the area of our booth (30 square metres / 320 square feet.) All of this in a brilliant high-resolution graphics headset powered by our super-duper Titan graphic card-equipped PC.

As for our simulator, as expected it is not going to work for the show. However, this is not entirely due to the fact that we have not had enough time to work on it yet, but because we have been given a standard US 110 volt power supply, yet we clearly specified in our requirements that we needed a 240 volts / 25 amps supply. Obviously, the minute we turn the thing on it draws a surge of power and the whole circuit trips out. The event organisers are really apologetic, they have messed up here and are trying to find a solution for us. Our simulator has been sponsored by the show organisers, none other than Unity3D themselves, so we have their logo plastered all over it. It would be a shame if we couldn't get it moving a bit.

The organisers have found a power convertor. It is supposed to convert the standard US 110 volts into 240 volts, but, after a few attempts, it is not going to work. On occasion, the simulator stays on for a few minutes but, eventually as it starts moving, it draws more amps and the whole thing trips again and again. Unfortunately for this event, the simulator will remain a static display and, while we had a large number of people coming to see it, nobody was able to sit in or try it. Admittedly, at the time the content was still very raw and the motion sync was very basic. It worked and the VR helmet was of great interest, but we would not have been able to provide a truly exciting experience even if we had had the power working properly

During the day, we also receive a link to our latest promotional video that our marketing company back home has put together. As they were still doing some edits before we left for the US, they told us they would send us the link on time to be displayed on the three large screens we have at our booth.

We all sit down around my laptop in the hotel's lobby and press the play button. It lasts one minute and 44 seconds and, as it ends, we all look at each other not quite sure what to say. We are disappointed!

It is a well put together video and has a good pace, but the problem we feel is that it barely showcases what we do. So, the decision is made that since I have my laptop with me and am capable of video editing, I am going to edit the video tonight before the event opens tomorrow. We all agree on what needs to be changed and we use various video clips that we have from our large selection to replace part of the video they have produced just in time before the event starts!

This is the morning of the first day of the event. We're all meeting up for breakfast down in the restaurant and, as I put on my new fancy Hackett London shirt for the first time, I realise it has these large cuff sleeves with no buttons that are designed for cuffs. Call me a little ignorant if you wish, but I'm not a suit-and-tie type of guy. The last time I wore a suit was at my wedding about 15 years before. I do have one black jacket in my wardrobe and a couple of ties, but as I am more of a casual wear type, I actually never wear it!

Since it is the first time I have worn cufflinks (no kidding!) I end up attaching them wrongly using my cufflink in the same way as a standard button. Of course – as I now know – the cuff sleeves need to be opposite and stick out. Stan explains that to me over the breakfast table and helps me attach my cufflinks to my shirts the right way round. I can't help but notice a slight look of embarrassment from James. He is "Mr Suit," always wearing a different suit and cufflinks, even during normal days in the office, so I think he is a little dismayed that I can be so ignorant about a piece of fashion. It is a small anecdote, but I wanted to mention it as you will see further in this book that James has a very large ego. While it had already been noticed by Paul and me, it was to become a very prominent issue in the near future!

MY FAVORITE QUOTE

"The ego is the single biggest obstruction to the achievement of anything."
Richard Rose –philosopher and author who studied human psychology, human weakness and human potential.

LESSON LEARNED:

I do like Mr Rose's quote, as I agree 110% with it!

The people who know me will tell you that I am the total opposite of an egocentric person. I do not need to be seen in fancy vehicles or posh hotels to boost my "rating" with other people, nor do I need to be eating at expensive restaurants or wearing branded clothing to boost my confidence.
I'm a strong believer that my attitude and my work speak for themselves. Being a competent and professional person at what I do, as well as having run my freelance business for several years with no marketing or advertising, essentially only getting work from word of mouth and recommendations, gives me the self-confidence I need.

However, as per the content of this chapter, we have started to establish that James is clearly an egocentric person and, as the remaining months unfold, it will become even more obvious that James' ego happens to be in the way in a lot of situations. Therefore, this quote fits this chapter.

WHAT WOULD YOU HAVE DONE?

1. Would you have travelled economy class and stayed at an average hotel saving around £10k?

2. Would you have travelled at least business class to help with the jet lag and been more productive on site, but stayed at cheaper hotels and saved around £5k?

3. Would you have travelled the way we did and stayed on site, which, although convenient, was more expensive?

Or maybe you would have done it completely differently? If so, please share what you would have done online at 1b1m1y.com

You can also log in to that website to view what other people would have done.

CHAPTER EIGHT

In the giant's playground

It's the 10th of February 2016. The first Vision Summit convention is now open! We have the largest stand of the whole convention! Across from us are Oculus showcasing their new CV1 (Customer Release) due out to the public in a couple of months. Three booths down are Google showcasing their Project Tango, a tablet capable of mapping a room, or part of it, and adding an AR character to it. In a separate private room, Microsoft are showcasing their new HoloLens AR headset to a select prebooked audience and, right to the side of us, there is this newcomer who is doing a lot of big marketing at the moment. Their name is going to become one of the most well known in VR – it's the HTC Vive.

It is interesting how far HTC have come since that day a few years ago. As far as I am aware, it was one of their first events showcasing their new Vive headset and they needed developers to produce content for it before it was released publicly later that year. Because of this, they decide to offer a free complete HTC Vive headset to every single attendee of the event, including exhibitors, so each one of us received ours a few weeks after returning home.

There are a lot of other new and lesser-known companies all around the convention hall, and it is busy – really busy! What is interesting is that it is mainly a professional and press event. Of course, anyone can attend, but VR is still very new and the majority of visitors are people who are either involved in some way with AR or VR, are tech geeks or are press teams from around the world covering the latest VR happenings.

We get interviewed for some UK and French websites and we get to meet lots of interesting people. We have a number of chats with individuals from movie studios as well as Sam, a board member of the Academy of Motion Picture Arts and Sciences (the same organisation that organises the famous Oscars ceremony.)

We have also been joined at our stand by Jimmy and Mark – our Liverpool studio colleagues – and they are now helping us deal with a phenomenal amount of visitors.

I don't know if it is busy because of the type of event we're at, or if it is our big booth and the F1 simulator that is attracting the crowds, but we do not seem to have any relief for the event's two-day duration.

One of the features of being a main sponsor of the event is that we have a 30-minute slot to talk in front of an audience of VR enthusiasts, not specifically about our company but more about the VR technology that we are working on and our plans for the future.

The team has selected me to do the talk! I've been writing my speech and rehearsing my timing on the flight over and I'm due to talk at 1pm. I leave my colleagues on the booth to handle the ever increasing flow of visitors and I head for the Ray Dolby Theatre which is located right next to the convention hall.

I don't know what to expect. I assumed it would be a small stage within the hotel for speakers to do their talks. However, as I step into the main auditorium, my heart nearly stops. There is this huge stage with two gigantic screens on each side and hundreds – maybe even thousands – of people in the enormous auditorium! Oh! Wasn't expecting that! I've never walked on such a big stage and in front of so many people before. My legs are shaking.

As a side note, the Dolby Theatre in Hollywood is where the Oscars ceremony is held every year, as well as the *America's Got Talent* TV programme, so it's a notoriously well-known location.

There is no time to ponder what ifs; the sound engineer is asking me to put on this wireless microphone kit, leads me backstage and explains to me how it is going to work.

"Your PowerPoint presentation will play on the two big screens on each side of the stage for spectators to view. You have a large monitor at your feet that will show you your next screen; you can control the flow with this hand remote. Next to the screen, there is a timer with the allocated time you have left, You must keep your presentation within that time or you will be cut off, as it is busy and there are more people after you. Also, stay within the white markers as two cameras are filming the presentation," I'm told.

There's a countdown from 10 and that's my cue to walk onstage and take it away. I'm shaking from head to toe and that can be heard in my voice as I'm starting to introduce myself to the huge audience. However, I crack on and, within a few minutes, the initial fear has rescinded and I am starting to feel a bit more at ease. I'm talking about our work, and about our plans to bring multiplayers in VR together as well as to develop a number of attractions based on motion and VR to provide the ultimate experience. The 30-minute presentation flies by, I take a few questions from the audience and it goes rather well. As I walk off the stage, there is a queue of about 15 people waiting to talk to me! Oh, I'm impressed and so pleased.

After a number of discussions with different people and companies – and exchanging contact details – I head back to our booth which is still rammed with people from every angle.

That's it, the show is over: time for a celebration drink! Not too much, though, as we have to start dismantling tonight because everything must be on its way by the end of tomorrow and we have a lot to move. After a few drinks together, we return to the convention hall and dismantle the whole booth, pack it up and get everything ready to be moved downstairs tomorrow morning before heading to bed.

Here's to another insane day of moving all our items one by one down to the unloading bay area the next day. Trusses, boxes of cameras and cables, flight cases with computers and network equipment, motion simulator, F1 chassis and lots of bits and pieces. By the end of the day, we have everything packed in the crates just in time as the shipping company lorry is there waiting for us to load the crates in. We wave them goodbye – the next time we'll see them is back home in a week or so.

As for us, we're flying back the following day, so it's finally time for a relaxing evening. We meet everyone at a smart steakhouse restaurant across from the hotel where we have our final meal in Hollywood, and a fair few beverages for some of us.

The next morning we're checking out as our return flight is in the early afternoon. The six rooms were pre-paid, so we've just got to settle the tabs which include the breakfast, the occasional lunch, a few dinners and a (fair) few bar drinks . . . Between the seven rooms, that's an $1,800 bill! "Ouch!" I wasn't expecting it to be that much. Anyway, Stan just hands me the company dollar credit card to settle the bill.

"Excuse me Sir, but that card is not going through," the reception clerk tells me!

"Are you sure? There should be more than enough balance. Can you try again?" I respond. The reception clerk kindly tries again, but still no luck so I have no choice but to settle the bill with my director's debit card which comes out of our British pound account. I'm not happy with this dollar credit card. How come it is not working? We had over $6,000 on it . . .

MY FAVORITE QUOTE

"The way to get started is to quit talking and begin doing."
Walt Disney –American entrepreneur, producer and founder of the Walt Disney Company.

LESSON LEARNED:

This quote is simple, yet so true in so many walks of life. How many times have you come across people who say they are going to do this, that or the other and yet nothing ever gets done?

Listening to these kinds of people is interesting, but having to deal with them is frustrating. I chose this quote because when we made the decision to attend this international event about two months ago, the list of things to do in order for us to be ready seemed unsurmountable. Yet we worked hard, very hard, we ticked every single box on that list and we arrived at the event as ready as we could have been.

Additionally, I remember quite clearly the look on the whole team's faces when we stood in the docking area in the unloading bay of the hotel looking at our crates and knowing we had to bring all of it, item by item, up two floors of lifts, corridors, standard doors and carpeted floors. It took seven people eight hours of hell, but we did it!

WHAT WOULD YOU HAVE DONE?

1. Would you have done what we did and be the biggest booth among the other big players there?

2. Would you have had a more discreet and smaller booth and just talked about the products but not display anything?

3. Would you have turned up as an attendee, gathered information and talked to people before showcasing the products?

Or maybe you would have done it completely differently? If so, please share what you would have done online at 1b1m1y.com

You can also log in to that website to view what other people would have done

CHAPTER NINE

Nearly halfway there!

We're back home. What a crazy eight days it has been! We're all exhausted, but it has been a rather successful event. James isn't too happy that our simulator wasn't working because of the power surge issues and is talking of suing Unity3D and the event technical people for the shambles. We have the requirements on paper and they have quite clearly failed to provide us with the necessary power supply.

One of the things I did when we got back was to investigate why our dollar card did not work and request to have the remaining funds returned to us.

"The card did not work because you only have $800 left on it," we are being told by the company that provided the card.

"Is this a joke? Where did the money go? It was only used by James to settle a couple of dinners and a few additional local purchases. We can't have spent over $6,000 in a matter of five days, can we?"

Well, looking at the receipts that James has brought back, although there are a few missing, it is quite clear there is nothing wrong with the card. It only got refused because the available credit simply had been spent and there wasn't enough left to settle the hotel balance.

I mention it to Paul who is not aware of the issue and he is definitely not impressed!

"Where has that money gone?" he asks.

"Well, I wasn't in possession of the card at all during our week in the US, since we spent the majority of our time working or exhibiting. The majority of the spending was on our room tabs, except for one evening when I decided to reward our young engineer's hard work with a steak meal. I actually settled this on my company's debit card, so I'm afraid we are going to have to raise this with James in our next meeting," I say to Paul.

We've been back for a week now and it is time for our board meeting. There is so much to cover. We need to review the Los Angeles event;

we need to discuss the lease proposal for the potential Liverpool studio; we need to agree the final headset designs so we can send them to print; we need to discuss recruitment of an additional software developer; and we also need to review and finalise the various new events that we have now booked for the next six weeks.

However, most importantly, we need to approve the legal terms for the planned loan note, as we now need our shareholders to release the second part of the investment money they promised initially. This is because we have spent over £300k in the last four months and we are now on our last £80k – hence the title for this chapter. This is just a formality, since it was already approved initially and the agreement has already been prepared, so James gets us to sign the paperwork and there it is – a new chunk of £440,000 is transferred to our business account.

Let's start with our Los Angeles event. Aside from the simulator issue, it went pretty well. We had a few minor hiccups with our headset, but we managed to showcase our tech and we had some very good meetings. We have a number of contacts that are very promising: one with the University of Lincoln in Nebraska who want to work with us to help us develop tech as well as use our technology for their students. There's good potential with Sam – our contact at the

Motion Picture Academy – who can see great potential for our technology in the entertainment industry. We also have a leading Hollywood architect for the rich and famous who is keen to use our technology, and we've also met with a couple of guys from Marvel Studios and have dozens of very interesting business contacts. So much so that James is suggesting we need to open an office in California!

This is not a bad idea, but who is going to manage it and does this mean we are going to spend more time in the USA? This could be detrimental to the company, as there is still a huge amount of development work in the coming months. Anyway, more on this in a few chapters!

Next on the agenda is the Liverpool studio. Following our recent trips there to visit the work sites and our discussion with the contractor and landlord, we now have a proposed lease contract. James is very keen to go ahead and lease one of the spaces to make it our first public VR studio. However, there are conflicting views between the three directors.

While Paul and I agree that it would be good to open a public studio, and having Mark and Jimmy's team next door to develop content and recommend it to their clients would be ideal, the unit that we have been looking at is on two floors. James is adamant that we need both floors and Paul is adamant that we only need one to start with. As for me, I'm kind of in the middle and would tend to agree with Paul: one floor is sufficient at the moment. But James has convincing arguments:

"We are going to put a simulator there as well and will put a design studio downstairs for architects."

"Yes, but who is going to run it? We are a two-hour flight away. What will happen when people need us there?" I query, but James reassures us.

"Not to worry. The guys next door will be able to handle all that and we will have a studio manager in place to oversee the running of it."

Still, something doesn't quite feel right. If we had known at the time the hassle this Liverpool studio was going to bring, we would have run a mile. Right now, however, it is the end of February and in exactly four and a half months it will be the grand opening of our Liverpool studio. We just don't know that yet.

Next: our headset designs. We've been working hard with a local designer to get our first headset professionally produced using 3D printed parts. We've had a number of parts printed locally recently and, after some adjustments, we feel it is ready to go for printing. (See photos page 166.)

We have decided to keep that first version as a professionally printed headset, as there are a couple of changes planned in our development. These will require small adjustments to the design so it will be easier to have a model that we can quickly alter but that still looks great when completed. The headset is going to look nice and we should then be on the final stage before having a production model.

Another small issue that needs to be resolved is what appears to be a salary mistake to the advantage of Stan. As we do not have a payroll system in place yet, I have been writing payslips manually for our staff, so at least everyone has something to go along with their monthly pay. While doing this, I've realised that Stan's salary is generously higher than what was initially agreed.

After clarification, James agrees that there has been a mistake and it will be corrected from now on. A mistake? It is a little odd, but at this stage of the business we have no reason to doubt him. However, as you will read in the coming chapters, this was one of the many events that led us to reinforce the nepotism status.

The next items on the agenda are the various events now booked for the coming months. In a couple of weeks, we've been invited to Birmingham for the largest Kitchen and Bathroom Show in the UK at the NEC (National Exhibition Centre.) This is a huge event and our business partner that we signed with back in December has booked us a 20 square metre (215 square feet) booth and is paying all our expenses to attend under their name.

They have just merged with a German company and are getting much bigger, so this is an amazing opportunity for us to retail our technology to interior designers across Europe.

After that four-day event, we will be heading straight down to London for the VR / AR wearable show, a new event held at the London ExCel. Then we have a few days back at base before we head down to Laval Virtual in France, an interesting event labelled as the largest VR event in the world, yet it is in a seriously remote part of rural France.

Finally, we are discussing going back to California very soon. Firstly because there are a number of contacts we need to follow up from our recent visit, secondly because we are looking to attend the SVVR (Silicon Valley VR,) which is a huge event happening in April in San Jose, and finally because James is seriously considering opening an office there. Located a few dozen miles south of San Francisco, San Jose is the epicentre of the Santa Clara Valley otherwise known as Silicon Valley where the majority of the world's largest tech companies are based.

There was so much to talk about during that very long board meeting that the extra spending on the dollar card nearly went unnoticed, but we did bring it up as being of concern and James is clear that it was money spent on entertaining some people he met who are crucial to the business' future. Looking at some of the receipts, we can't fail to notice that a lot of their "entertainment" has been on drinks, including a bottle of champagne at $500! I wonder if that is going to bring about anything worthwhile.

After the long board meeting, Paul and I decide to have a catch-up as there are a number of things we feel uncomfortable with. Things are happening that we do not seem to have much of a decision on, and there are huge sums of money that have been spent in the last few months which we are not happy with.

Don't get me wrong, we have made joint decisions for the majority of the money that we spent on things like the motion platform, the F1 replica, the design of the headsets, new additional motion capture cameras and a good range of computer hardware. So far this has cost over £120k, but those are now assets of the company and are beneficial to the development of our products, while the other £180k has essentially been spent on travelling, entertainment, lawyer and accountant fees (already in excess of £45K between those two,) rebranding and marketing and attending and sponsoring events.

I am not trying to make excuses; I fully accept that I am an executive director and it is the responsibility of me and Paul to put our foot down if we are not happy with certain things within the company. However, all I can say is that Paul and I feel a little pressurised. After all, James brokered the investment deal for us, he comes from an investment background and has a couple of successful investments under his belt. Shareholders are trusting him with a very large sum of their own money, so, company directors or not, are we competent enough to challenge his decisions? Maybe he knows better and we should stick to what we know – which is technology.

It is interesting, as with hindsight I can look back now and confidently say that these first doubts should have been sufficient for me and Paul to put a stop to it and call an EGM. But we did not, and we continued.

If we had called an EGM at the time, maybe things would have turned out differently. In any case, we still had some time to alter the course of the company, but not a lot. In fact, in about two months from then, it would be too late. The fate of the company was going to be sealed and it was going to close down whatever happened.

Yet it took me another five months before serious actions took place. Ah . . . hindsight. What a magic word!

MY FAVORITE QUOTE

"Money is like gasoline during a road trip. You don't want to run out of gas on your trip, but you're not doing a tour of gas stations."
Tim O'Reilly – founder, and CEO of O'Reilly Media.

LESSON LEARNED:

Now that's a quote that states the obvious.

What is interesting is that this quote is actually to the point, but too many businesses seem to forget that – we certainly did! As a person who has never been extravagant in what I spend and nor is Paul, the amount of money that our company had spent was a great cause of concern already. However, our lack of knowledge when it came to running corporate companies meant we ended up trusting the person with the "financial knowledge" and position.

I have run businesses before and since Vizuality, and during a previous business tenure I had to travel a lot, but I never felt the need to indulge in expensive hotels, business class or luxury items.

In the past, when I managed to clear a good profit from my company, that was money I could choose to either pay as dividend or reinvest in the company and use it as I saw fit. But spending large sums of money which the company had not earned yet did not seem appropriate.

WHAT WOULD YOU HAVE DONE?

1   In that board meeting, would you have
    stepped up, put your foot down and
    challenged James' decisions and started
    setting spending limitations?

2   Would you have called an EGM and
    established the decision-making once
    and for all, at the risk of creating a
    serious, irreparable break in the
    director/shareholder relationship?

3   Would you have done what we did
    which essentially was to express that we
    were not in agreement, but somehow
    ended up going ahead with it as we were
    not a strong enough voice?

Or maybe you would have done it completely
differently? If so, please share what you would
have done online at 1b1m1y.com

You can also log in to that website to view what
other people would have done

CHAPTER TEN

Copyright, patents and trademarks

As I previously mentioned, our accountant and lawyer bills had already been mounting up quite seriously, but that was nothing compared to what was to come. It is the end of February and one of the very rare occasions when Paul and I end up meeting our lawyer in order to discuss how to handle the company's various intellectual properties.

Now you probably know already but if not, I just want to clarify that the intellectual property of a company is what makes it valuable; it's what constitutes the uniqueness of the business. It protects our ideas, designs, concepts and developments and it also protects people and clients against copy or imitations. But, more crucially, it's what makes the company valuable to investors and it's what establishes the value of the company so shareholders have a return on their investment. As such, this is a vital process for the company.

Our first lawyer meeting is for the wireless headset. Although we designed our headset using existing technology that we altered to work for our purpose, what we did was relatively unique at the time and that, according to our patent lawyer, is enough to warrant a patent application.

We also discuss the opportunity of trademarking our company name, logo and product names, so, once registered, we can use the registered trademark symbol (®) and protect our identity.

A few weeks later, we have another meeting in relation to our VR helmet. Again, we didn't invent anything there, but what we did was design and put together a number of off-the-shelf items to serve a new and specific purp̃e. According to our lawyer, it's all down tǫ detailed description of the purpose s⸗ should be patentable.

ᵎber of
Paul and I have to prepar⸗scribing our detailed documents esseᵣ⸗ designs and software developmentᵗ⸗ instructions for our processes, as well ą̃

headsets. We also have to provide a list of planned content development stories so they can be copyrighted. I understand that this has limited benefits; it is for the safety factor more than anything else.

Paul and my attendance at those meetings are essentially from a technical point of view to provide the specifications and answer our lawyer's questions in relation to the different functionalities and limitations of the products and designs so he can draft a suitable search document to submit the patent and trademark searches. "The searches and approval of the trademark and patents could take a while," we are told by our lawyer. "But in the meantime, it will have a patent-pending status, so it is protected from now on."

After those meetings, we actually never met the lawyer again. James was handling that and all we know is that we are using the registered ext to our business name and that everything is in nd.

Wh
Vizualit as been made clear by James is that hence th oking for further investments, structure, tion of the multi-companies implemente hares and the legally legal agreeme ments, loan notes and other in place by our lawyers at

James' request, as well as the patents and trademarking process.

However, there are another couple of important steps that our young company needs to complete in order to receive further investment offers. Namely, a short, clean and professional pitch deck that should entice investors to put their money in our company; a good business plan for the next two to three years; and, ideally, a strong financial forecast. However, in such a young company with so many things on the boil, producing an accurate financial forecast is pretty much impossible. Anyway, these are the types of documents expected by investors.

So how did we fare in producing those documents? Not that great, actually. I clearly recall a phrase James must have said to me and Paul at least half a dozen times,
"I'm going to lock myself in a dark room for a week and produce the business plan, forecast and pitch deck."

Being the financial director and the one who clearly came from the investment world that the only person who could provide with the pitch properly, so Paul and I offered facts about deck in order to provide James to produce our technology and plan. the forecast and

Unfortunately, James never locked himself in that dark room and never produced a pitch deck or a proper forecast. He did, however, produce a business plan, but it was more of a "Company History" than anything else.

Considering the above, what do you think our chances are of receiving an offer of investment? Most people would be correct in saying "very small," wouldn't they? Well, actually, we did better than expected!

It is obvious by now that I am blaming James for our various shortfalls as well as the excessive and unnecessary spending. Of course, this is solely my view and, like any situation in life, there are two sides to every story. I'm sure James would have his own arguments and reasons in answer to those points.

However, the other person I do hold responsible is me. You see, I am not the type of person to shy away from my responsibilities. If I ha... messed something up, I am the first one to put... hand up, admit it and take the blame. On this o... interest... on, I should have taken a stronger ready an... king sure the documents were down for th... ced, as well as putting my foot to affect the ...us other matters that started ...s' relationships.

Over the last couple of years, I have discussed this experience with several different people. Some have argued that each and every director has a task to accomplish, and that delegation and trust in each others' capabilities is paramount. After all, if everyone gets involved in each others' business, then it becomes an inefficient company.

On the other hand, some people have told me that company board meetings are designed to discuss every decision and address any issues or problems, especially crucial ones so that things do not degenerate before it is too late.

MY FAVORITE QUOTE

"Always look for the fool in the deal. If you don't find one, it's you."
Mark Cuban – AXS TV chairman and entrepreneur.

LESSON LEARNED:

Mr Cuban's quote is an interesting one. Let's be honest: in every walk of life there are lots of people who talk the talk, but who don't walk the walk. In any business deal, the chance that there will be one is quite high.

In this instance, while I accept that I should have stepped up and queried what was happening with the business plan and pitch deck, at the end of the day, James fits Mr Cuban's quote perfectly. James could certainly talk well and did come across as an assertive and knowledgeable director, but, when it came to action, there was very little of it.

WHAT WOULD YOU HAVE DONE?

1. Do you believe in delegation and trust in each other as directors? Do you believe that each person is going to do their tasks without having to go over them in detail at each board meeting and having to report what has or has not been done?

2. Or, do you believe that there should be a detailed communication and processes system in place where every director reports on their own progress, completed tasks and other duties? These are then reviewed at board meetings between directors which is where any non-completed tasks are discussed and addressed.

Or maybe you would have done it completely differently? If so, please share what you would have done online at 1b1m1y.com

You can also log in to that website to view what other people would have done

CHAPTER ELEVEN

Do it yourself

It's the middle of March 2016. We've just returned from back-to-back events. The first one was the four-day KBB event at Birmingham NEC (National Exhibition Centre,) together with our kitchen designer partner. It was a lot of hard work, as since we are one of the first to offer VR visualisation, we had a lot of interest.

It was followed by our VR / AR Wearable Tech Event at the London ExCel. We were joined once again by our colleagues from Liverpool who had their own display right next to us showcasing some of their AR tech. As a side anecdote, while Paul and I are getting rather good at setting up our motion tracking rig now, at that particular event it took us over seven hours to get it set up and working. First, due to some skylight windows that were shining sunlight straight down on our booth and then a new issue took us a couple of hours to identify: the infrared light of the cameras was reflecting onto the chrome part of the booth barriers and was affecting the markers' detection.

We are all glad that both events are over as we're exhausted! We are now back to base for a few days before leaving for France for the big Laval Virtual event. Two weeks after that, we are heading back west to Silicon Valley for the SVVR and the VR Arcade Conference.

Although it is interesting to attend these events, showcase our technology, speak to like-minded people and make business opportunities, the problem of being on the move so much for the last four weeks and for the next four weeks is that our development process has slowed right down.

However, the benefit of these events is that our wireless headset has now been road tested with lots of people. The feedback is good and our concept is certainly drawing crowds.

Our team is growing. We have now been joined by Frank, our new developer. It's not easy for him to join us at this particular time, as there is so much to do and so little time to get him adjusted. He is literally thrown in at the deep end. Thankfully, he is professional and adjusts quickly to what we do and our chaotic way of working at the moment.

I have decided to allocate him the task of completing the F1 simulator motion algorithm and integration with the content. At this stage, the motion simulator is working well, but the content is not yet up to scratch and the motion is not always perfectly in sync. There is also the overall setting control panel to do, the end user interface to control the experience and dozens of small tweaks to make the experience truly outstanding.

As the lead developer for the company, I spend a fair bit of time with Frank to brief him on what I am expecting from him, what the whole simulator concept is about and what it needs to achieve. As a self-sufficient and proactive individual, he grasps it pretty quickly and, for the next couple of months, Frank and Mikey are left to work a lot on their own to improve the simulator.

Talking of our F1 simulator, James has asked me to order a full second simulator to be installed at the Liverpool studio. That's a second full six DOF (Degrees of Freedom) motion platform and, this time, a full-length F1 replica chassis (see photos page 164) as well as accessories such as a steering wheel and pedals, tracking cameras and a new VR helmet.

Paul is not in agreement! He says that we are spending a lot of money already, this is going to put another £60k dent in our fast melting funds and we could maybe move our development simulator temporarily to Liverpool.

James, however, is categoric. The Liverpool studio needs that simulator, this is going to be our first studio and we have to make a serious impact. The press will be there and this will draw crowds and attract interest.

As for me, well, since we ended up signing the two floors and since I am a bit biased towards the F1 simulator as it is ultimately my baby, I go along with James' idea and – here we are – another £60k chunk of money gone. However, our company's assets are growing and this will be the main Liverpool simulator.

It is now the end of March. As we were not able to find a ferry to France, and as the Laval Virtual Exhibition is located in the middle of very rural France, James has organised for us to fly over in a private jet. Six of us, 45 minutes flying time, one-way flight – £3,000.

We've arrived in Laval, a tiny rural town about two hours west of Paris. Thanks to some incredible marketing and fabulous organisation, this event has become known all over the world as far as VR and AR is concerned.

For the five-day duration of the event, the biggest names in VR and AR are exhibiting and thousands of visitors will come from all over the world. We have a big booth right by the entrance, our stand setup goes well and we are almost ready. Unfortunately, unbeknownst to us, our F1 simulator is going to become an issue again. After being fully set up and drawing a crowd before the event is even open, we power up our simulator and – bang! The power to our booth and a few others around us goes off. What happened?

The event's electrical team arrives, resets the power and we try again. Sure enough –bang! – and it all goes off again.

"You can't turn it back on," say the event's electrician. "Your platform is shorting the electrical block." We are miffed! What happened? It was working fine up to a week ago before it left our studio.

Thankfully, the local electrician team is very friendly and offer to help us by looking at the simulator electrical block and testing it to see what is wrong. After about 15 minutes they tell us that everything is fine.

"There is nothing wrong with the simulator; however, it is drawing a lot of amps when it starts up," the electrician explains.

"Yes, we know that. We clearly advised that we need a 240 volt / 25 amp supply for it."

"Yes, you do," confirms the electrician. "But in France – unlike the UK – systems are protected via a fuse box. Plug sockets aren't protected, so if too much voltage is drawn in one go, it will trip the whole fuse circuit as a safety measure."

What we need is a large voltage regulator / UPS unit so the current drawn is constant while the regulator handles the power surges required by the simulator. As it is late in the day, and the show opens the next morning, it is too late to source a local power regulator.

We do not know that, so we are left yet again with a non-working simulator. James isn't happy and neither am I, but what can we do? James asks us to take it all down,

"We can't have a simulator on our booth that is not working again," he says.

I'm not entirely in agreement about that. While I would, of course, prefer to be able to show a working simulator, even with selected pre-briefed users, the simulator is such a crowd puller that since it is now fully installed, why not showcase it as our upcoming attraction?

It may not move, but we can certainly sell the concept – and I can assure you that I can sell the concept very well as I absolutely love the whole idea and experience. In my view, it could even be beneficial, as people understand that this is brand-new tech and are more accepting if things don't work perfectly initially. I feel it would make them even more keen to keep in touch and be informed on progress.

But no, James is having none of it. The simulator is dismantled and pulled to the back of the loading bay where I have organised for our shipper to come and pick it up early.

Aside from that issue, the event goes well. We have a few issues with interferences on our wireless headset, but, thankfully, our backup "emergency" headset does us proud and we manage to handle the whole event nicely. It is yet another successful event.

As far as business opportunities are concerned, we have met Mr Dong – CEO of a large Shanghai-based event company. He asks James and me to sit down with him to discuss a potential distribution partnership.

He likes our products very much and wants to know more about pricing, requirements and whether his company could distribute our products in China!

We have also met Francois, a French man representing the interest of the CNES (Centre National d'Étude Spatiale) or, in English, the French Space Agency! They have developed a technology that he feels could be of interest to us, but I'll tell you more about this in a couple of chapters.

We have also met Nick and Steven, two brothers who are in the process of opening a large VR arcade in Rennes, a city only an hour away from Laval which has a large student community.

And we have also gathered several other contacts and opportunities which we will be dealing with on our return to base.

It's early April now. We've only been back from Laval for a few days and we are getting ready for our return trip to the USA.

James, Paul and Stan are going ahead one week before me, to Los Angeles initially, to follow up on leads from the previous US trip as well as to look at a few possible locations for our LA office. I am meeting them in San Francisco, where we are holding two big events.

I've got a huge amount of work to do over the coming two weeks before our trip to the US. Firstly, we've just received our new headset parts fresh from 3D printing. It does not all fit perfectly well, but it is looking good (see photos page 164) so we need to assemble them as we are intending to have our new commercial headset ready to showcase at our next event.

We have also received our new headset wireless transmission boards. Due to the limitation and potential interferences of the 60Ghz frequency we have been experiencing on regular occasions, we have switched to using the more standard 5Ghz frequency. However, without going into too much technical detail, this means using a different way of transmitting the data as the bandwidth has far less capacity, but it is also far more flexible as it allows many more frequencies together meaning more people at the same time.

It also allows connection without line of sight which, for what we do is, very important. The biggest benefit is that it is far more lenient to interferences.

The new frequency, however, has a small but important drawback. It increases the latency by around 10ms (milliseconds) so where we were at about 25ms with our current headset, we will be reverting back to around 30-35ms.

Finally, I've also got to extend and fine-tune some of our VR content, as our booth at the SVVR is going to be the biggest so far with 60 square metres (650 square feet) for our tracking studio alone. Our existing content – although capable of handling this larger area – has been designed for a smaller booth size.

We now have three good contents that we are showcasing to everyone. This means a fair few hours of editing are required to adjust and improve them so they make the most out of the larger booth.

The first of our content is called the Haunted Manor. This is a very popular one with multi-room exploration using our now traditional flashlight. A lift allows the user to "go downstairs" and reuse the same VR space to explore more areas.

The second content is our fast-paced Moon-based Station 2020. Having returned to the moon, the human race located in the brand-new Moon-based Station are attacked by a bunch of unfriendly aliens and the idea is to use the laser gun we provide to get rid of them and walk out of the base to escape.

Finally, our third and best content to date is set in the middle of a desert. Following a plane crash, the user comes across an odd abandoned temple and uses our flame torch to explore it and find help. To make the experience lifelike, we have created a realistic looking handheld torch that users can move around to light up the room. With this content, we have just started to experiment with reusable floor space. We get the users to walk around and around the temple visiting several different areas and rooms without ever realising that, in real life, they are going over their own steps. This makes the content seem huge to them.

MY FAVORITE QUOTE

"Success seems to be connected with action. Successful people keep moving. They make mistakes, but they don't quit."
Conrad Hilton –Hotelier and founder of the Hilton Hotel Chain.

LESSON LEARNED:

Mistakes! Who doesn't make them? The main thing when mistakes are made is to keep moving, learn from them, rectify the problem and try again. We've had a few hiccups recently: the simulator not working at events, the headset transmission not always being reliable and our tracking system needing adjustments to be more performant and accurate. Some of those hiccups were mistakes, some were lack of experience and some were due to bad luck. This can take its toll on you, especially when you work very hard to achieve something.

In our case, we never dropped our focus. We fixed the headset, we sourced an alternative wireless transmission solution and worked to develop our very own LED-based active marker tracking solution to improve the optical tracking.

WHAT WOULD YOU HAVE DONE?

1. Would you have not booked so many events and focused on developing the products in hand to make them better before showing them to the public?

2. Would you have done what we did: go and attend lots of events, showcase the technology – even when it wasn't perfect or working – so as to expose the company to the tech world and get feedback from users trying our technology (which, at the time, was pretty revolutionary?)

Or maybe you would have done it completely differently? If so, please share what you would have done online at 1b1m1y.com

You can also log in to that website to view what other people would have done

CHAPTER TWELVE

If you fail to prepare, prepare to fail

It's the 14th of April. Paul, James and Stan are about to fly to Los Angeles and there is some tension between us three directors. During the nine weeks since we attended our first event in Los Angeles, we have been on the road for half of that time so we are all exhausted. This doesn't help, but there is more to it than that.

Paul and I tend to agree on the majority of things, but James seems to want to have his own way on a lot of decisions or matters needing attention, whether or not Paul and I agree. In some cases, James has not even consulted us before making the decision.

As James and Stan are ready to fly out to London to connect to their US flight, they will join Paul who happens to be in London already for personal reasons. Paul is staying at a Premier Inn Hotel not far from Heathrow Airport while, once again, James and Stan are staying at the airport's Sofitel. This leads to an argument about money being spent unnecessarily again.

As for me, since my aim is to have as much time as possible at base to fit in as much work as I can before the events, and since I am going to fly straight to San Francisco, I ask Stan – who organised the last round of travel to the US – to count me out. I will sort out my flight to find the most suitable – last minute – one myself.

Considering that I am making my booking quite late and since it is the Easter holidays, the prices of business class flights are stupidly high, so I decide to book myself onto a premium economy. I cannot justify the £3,000+ price and, to be honest, it doesn't make any difference as I am so tired I sleep most of the flight anyway!

After an 11-hour flight, I arrived at San Francisco Airport. It takes me a little while to clear US immigration this time, but eventually I come out of the International Terminal, jump into an Uber and I'm making my way down to the Hilton Hotel in San Jose where we are staying. This is only a 30 or so minute drive from the airport, but a very interesting one especially if you are a bit of a tech geek like me. This 40-mile stretch of road crosses Redwood City, Palo Alto and Santa Clara. During the ride, you can spot the majority of the biggest tech company headquarters in the world, such as Oracle, Google, Intel, Adobe, Cisco, PayPal, Tesla, Apple, HP and Facebook.

We chose the Hilton Hotel located on Almaden Boulevard in the heart of San Jose as it is located right across the road from the San Jose Convention Centre where the SVVR is taking place. Once checked in and refreshed, I go down to the hotel's bar and meet up with everyone. They have just flown in from Los Angeles on an internal flight. After a few minutes, Paul pulls me to the side and explains what a waste of time that week in Los Angeles has been!

They did go and see three or four studio spaces but, according to Paul, it was either not suitable or a pointless exercise. There were also a few short catch-up meetings, but otherwise it was a well "lubricated" trip for both James and Stan.

Considering that Paul is not a big drinker and as this was now our fifth trip together in a little more than two months, this did not surprise me. Both Paul and I had grown quite used to these James and Stan party nights before, during and after the events.

As previously mentioned, Paul and I were not overly enthusiastic about the opening of our first studio in Liverpool, essentially because it is a two-hour flight away from our base among other things. However, we were convinced, went ahead with the idea and signed the lease. As far as having a US studio, however, at this stage Paul and I are not even entertaining the idea.

If there was a decent purpose or opportunity on the table, then yes. However, considering that this seems to be just another way to show off again, we are completely cold at the idea of spending even more money for no real reason. We leave the discussion at that and move on to the many other things that need attention. The outcome is that this was the last time we ever heard of the idea of opening a studio in California. I'm not sure if James changed his mind, or realised that he would struggle to get us on his side for this. Maybe he figured out that this was going to cost a small fortune and dilapidate our remaining funds even more than they were already. Who knows?

It is now the 24th of April. We are in California for two weeks, first for the SVVR in three days' time and then for the VR Arcade Conference – another brand-new event. This is held at the Computer History Museum located in Mountain View right behind the Microsoft campus and only a few miles away from San Jose.

I am looking after the VR Arcade Conference with Stan while James and Paul fly to Lincoln in Nebraska. We have been invited by Lincoln University to discuss a potential partnership both from their side as they would like to get their students to help with developments on our wireless VR and tracking technology, but also from the commercial side of us becoming a supplier to their establishment.

That's the second university we are dealing with now. We have already established an agreement with Portsmouth University back in the UK. There is also some interest in linking up the two establishments.

As a side note, this is in early 2016 and our discussions with those two prestigious universities have been focused on trying to link them up together in VR. The aim is for each of them to have one of our motion VR studios with students and teachers collaborating in a common VR environment while being thousands of miles apart. This is an incredible opportunity for the company, both in terms of future developments that the universities can contribute to, but also from a marketing and reputation aspect.

To my knowledge, there are now some VR multiuser collaboration options available, but the kind of full-scale, multiuser, motion tracked collaboration we planned is yet to be done even three years on.

We start to set up on the 26th as the event room was not available earlier, but we did check the day before that all our equipment had arrived and everything was ready for us to get cracking first thing in the morning.

Our booth is huge, a total of 84 square metres (900 square feet) with three quarters of it reserved for our motion capture studio, the biggest we've had so far. Oh – and guess what? We are the major sponsor of the event. I can't recall the cost exactly, but I'm pretty sure it was an extra £10k.

I suspect that most of you will agree that it was another extravagant and unnecessary cost, as per Paul and I. I'm also pretty sure James would argue back questioning whether Eddy – who is mentioned a bit further down – would have called us at all had we not been sponsoring the event! An interesting fact is that the two other companies we identified as our main competitors – VRcade who we spoke with initially over a year ago and remain in touch with and Zero Latency – are nowhere to be seen. I wonder why they are choosing not to showcase their technology at such a big event.

It's late afternoon. Paul and I have managed to put up our huge booth in record time (see photos page 165) while the Velcro Team are still finishing their job.

Since you might be wondering, the Velcro Team is the name Paul and I have given to James and Stan, as all they seem to do at our events is stick Velcro to the truss structure and attach the company banners and then disappear while we are left to adjust the banners as, most of the time, they are not properly placed.

On that day, as Paul and I are finishing the calibration of our studio and the wireless communication tests, we notice that two of our huge banners, hung by James and Stan, look absolutely rubbish. One is creased very badly and the other is damaged and has black marks on it. We intervene and say politely to James that we can't use those banners as they do not look professional.

James insists that we need the banners in order to promote the business and make the booth look more finished, but Paul and I assert that it doesn't look right for the company image to display them.

With these words, James throws his toys out of his pram and walks out of the room. We do not see him again until much later that day. This gives us both a good giggle, as we have had a few of these tantrums before when things didn't quite go James' way. In a board meeting, he would throw his pen on the table or kick things off.

The next day is the show opening day. We're all set to go and everything starts well, however, as things get busy, our headset starts to misbehave. The wireless communication keeps cutting off and the display is very fuzzy. What is going on now? We try several of our other headsets (as we are now travelling with at least four,) but the results are the same.

I quickly assess that it must be down to interferences. This event is held in a cavernous warehouse with hundreds and hundreds of visitors, all with smartphones. Additionally, the booth across from us is a new VR company showing their wireless controller that works with a strong magnetic field. Could it be that this is creating interferences with our 60Ghz band?

After a couple of hours of having issues and trying various trial and error solutions, we assess that if we walk out of the event room the headset works fine. It's when we walk back in that the issues start again. There is no way to know for sure the reasons for the issue, but it is quite clearly happening when we are inside the event room and, as such, likely due to interferences we have not experienced before.

At this stage, I decide to run back to the hotel. We have in our bags our new wireless transmission boards and, while we have never used them publicly before, I have no choice but to give them a go. Within a few minutes, my hotel room desk has become a workshop. Dremel kit, soldering iron, glue gun – I am removing the current wireless transmission board from two of our headsets and replacing it with our new one. They are of similar sizes and the way we have designed the headset means I can fit them in the same place; however, the wiring is different, and this requires a fair bit of soldering and a little gluing to keep things together. It's not ideal, but it is the only solution I have right now. It takes me nearly two hours to get the headsets changed over, I then run back to the event room where Paul has pretty much given up with the remaining headsets and is talking to people instead.

We connect the new transmitters to the PCs, we power up the headset and – Hooray! – it is working. Our new wireless boards have connected almost instantly and the graphics are of incredibly high quality. The only small issue that we are aware of is that, due to the different transmission protocol used, these headsets have slightly more latency than our other headsets.

We're only talking around 10ms more, so it's not a huge difference, but, as I'm so used to our headsets, I immediately notice it. However, nobody who tries our content over the SVVR or the following VR Arcade event mentions anything and, in fact, the feedback is great.

We do have plans to improve this, but this is such an enhancement that these new headsets are going to become our official ones shortly after our return.

I chose this chapter's title essentially because I am someone who tries to plan everything in every detail. While it is not always possible to think of every eventuality, I tend to take extra bits and pieces with me including gaffer tape and glue guns so, if problems arise, I've got tools I can use to find a solution.

On more than one occasion, this approach has been very useful, but in this particular event it was a blessing. While we missed three-quarters of the first day, we certainly made up for it over the following two days and it then went really well.

Mr Dong – the Shanghai-based CEO we met in France – comes back to see us again and tries our technology several times. This time it's official: he wants his company – BroadMesse – to become a distributor of our technology in China. James is meeting up with Mr Dong in a hotel nearby to discuss the details.

We have also met with Igor and his brother. They are two Indonesian businessmen and really like what we have showcased to them. They share their plans to open a large VR arcade in Jakarta initially, but to expand across South East Asia. They think our technology is perfectly suited for them.

We didn't know then that they would become our first – and only – client.

On the first day of the event, I also get a call on my mobile from Eddy. He is from Oppenheimer – the technology investment bank – and would like to come to see us the next day and speak to us about what we do.

MY FAVORITE QUOTE

"If you can push through that feeling of being scared, that feeling of taking a risk, really amazing things can happen."
Marissa Mayer – president and CEO of Yahoo!.

LESSON LEARNED:

Let me tell you that as the SVVR event opened its doors and our headsets started to misbehave, my heart sank into my shoes. We had the biggest booth of all, we were major sponsors and if none of our headsets were working, we would have had to talk our way around with people for three days. It would have looked pretty bad.

Who knows, maybe we would not even have had the deal with Mr Dong or the meeting with Eddy from Oppenheimer if our headsets had not eventually started working.

As I was reconfiguring the headsets to use our new transmission board in my hotel bedroom, my hands were shaking and I kept repeating over and over in my head, "Come on. This has to work. We can't fail now, we've come too far." To repeat some words from my chosen quote, "I was scared, very scared" when this happened and, "it was a risk" to go away from the booth for a couple of hours and change the headset to the new transmission board we hadn't even tested in public. That risk paid off, though, and the rest of the show – as well as the following one – turned out to be great.

WHAT WOULD YOU HAVE DONE?

1. Do you think that going a week early to Los Angeles for three people travelling business class and staying in a nice hotel to look at potential studio locations for our company was a potentially good idea and could have been beneficial to the company?

2. Or do you think that this was a total waste of time and more importantly, a waste of money?

Or maybe you would have done it completely differently? If so, please share what you would have done online at 1b1m1y.com

You can also log in to that website to view what other people would have done

CHAPTER THIRTEEN

The three million dollar opportunity

Eddy comes to see us at our booth. I get him to try our Haunted Mansion and we show him a video we made of our F1 simulator that we are also presenting. After a short discussion, he asks if we could reconvene that afternoon in a meeting room to discuss things quietly in more details?

As one of the main sponsors of the event, we have our own on-site private meeting room which is very handy for these types of meetings. James, Eddy and I head to the room while Stan and Paul stay on the booth to assist visitors.

Eddy starts by explaining that he is the assistant of Michael, an investment manager at Oppenheimer, and that he has been following us, seen what we do and would like to discuss possible investment if we are interested!

Yes, of course we are interested!

James takes over initially on the financial side as this is more his field. He explains the seed funding the company has received so far, how the company and our shareholdings are structured and our financial plans for the future. After a little while, I take over and explain our two main products, why we are different, where we feel large-scale VR is going and the different roads we can explore with our technology, as well as some of the opportunities we already have in progress.

Eddy remains stoic. It is difficult to know what he is thinking, as he does not let his feelings show.

After listening to us for about an hour and a half, Eddy asks us for our pitch deck. "Sorry!" responds James. "We haven't got the pitch deck with us, but we can provide it to you on our return to base."

As the meeting is ending, Eddy excuses himself and calls his manager Michael. They have a short conversation and Eddy turns around to us and says, "We're interested in taking this further. Could you come over to our head office in downtown San Francisco for a formal discussion together with my manager Michael?"

Since James and Paul are heading to Nebraska immediately after SVVR, we decide that I will go over to the Oppenheimer head office the day after the VR Arcade event and James and Paul will join us in a conference call.

After three busy days and hundreds of visitors trying out our tech (see photos page 165) we end the SVVR in a rather cheerful mood, albeit with a few initial issues. Overall the event has been a pretty successful one and we have a few exciting opportunities lined up.

We dismantle everything on that same afternoon and our local shipping company is already there – right on time – to collect our 200kg of exhibition equipment and take it about 20 miles up the road to the Computer History Museum in Mountain View.

We are having a day off in between the two events, so we all head up to San Francisco by train. James is taking us to the Franciscan Crab Restaurant on Fisherman's Wharf Pier 43. This is an idyllic location. The restaurant is right by the sea opposite Alcatraz Island where the infamous prison – now a visitor attraction – sits. To the left-hand side, there is the huge Golden Gate Bridge which San Francisco is known for.

The restaurant is nice, busy but nice, and so is the bill at over $300 for a lunch for four! After this rather expensive meal, we order an Uber and travel across the Golden Gate Bridge to the small city of Sausalito. We stop at the Barrel House Tavern located right next to the ocean with the whole of San Francisco in the background. What an amazing setting!

After a few beverages sitting on the terrace with the waves of the San Francisco Bay at our feet, Sam – the gentleman with the Motion Academy connection we met in LA in February – joins us. James has been in regular contact with him.

As this is his hometown, he takes us around a couple of other places for a few more drinks and then to his friend's place back in downtown San Francisco. This is a rather big house along one of those steep San Francisco hills and there are a fair few people there who we don't know!

We introduce ourselves and discuss our technology and our company, but, as the party mood increases, we eventually say goodbye and return to our hotel.

The next day, Paul and James are flying to Nebraska, while Stan and I are setting up at the Computer Museum for the two-day event. We are staying at the Crowne Plaza in Palo Alto which is only four miles away from the venue.

I really like Palo Alto, it is such a nice city: modern, with beautiful parks and home to the famous Stanford University.

The event goes well. It's not really busy, but I have a couple of interesting meetings. On the final day, I start to help Stan dismantle everything, but I need to head to downtown San Francisco for our Oppenheimer meeting.

The Uber driver drops me right at the bottom of the Oppenheimer Tower. I'm a little early, but it's all good. The reception warden gets the lift – which has no buttons – for me and takes me directly to the 25th floor.

Eddy is there, welcomes me in and introduces me to Michael. I am led to a huge boardroom overlooking San Francisco. The plan is that I was to come an hourly early with one of our headsets and our marketing material so I could brief Eddy and Michael in more detail about what we are working on. Later, James and Paul will join us for a conference call.

That hour went really quickly. I always enjoy talking about our tech and our projects, and Michael and Eddy seem very interested. I can tell by the questions they are asking that they know a fair bit about VR and tech. Then, James joins us in a conference call alongside Paul who is with him in Nebraska.

First, we discuss similar topics to the ones we covered with Eddy a few days earlier, but this time for Michael's benefit. Then, Michael takes a turn to talk and tells us,

"Guys, you have a great business, a great concept and some great plans. That makes you the type of company we like to invest in. What are you looking for?"

James goes on to explain a little more about the forecast and various financial returns and then announces that "we" are looking for an 18-20million-dollar investment . . .

A few seconds of total silence follows.

I've put the "we" in speech marks as I am not entirely sure where James got this figure from. It should really read "James."

The last couple of times James, Paul and I discussed investments, James said that our company value would be around £10million (about $12million,) but we never really expanded on the subject.

Realistically, this is a subjective figure since we have not had any sales yet and our value is essentially our ideas, designs, patents and future plans. I remember discussing this with Paul a few times before and querying,

"How can we be worth so much already and on what basis? Is this a figure James has plucked from the air or are there any proper formulas used to work this out?"

Anyway, I am now at the top of the Oppenheimer head office in a boardroom with Michael and Eddy plus James and Paul on a conference call. Michael readjusts himself on his seat after nearly falling off it at that heavy investment request from James. The whole blue sky atmosphere seems to have switched over to grey and windy!

"Well," starts Michael. "As this is your Series A funding, we would rarely invest much more than $5million. On this occasion, we were more thinking of an offer around $2.5-$3million."

I am shaking. I'm sitting across the table from Michael and I can see his expression and attitude. He is genuinely offering us a $2.5-$3million investment. This is amazing, I'm thinking. I'm very much aware that our initial investment is melting like snow under the sun with now nearly £600k of our budget gone, so this is coming at a perfect time. It will allow us to produce injection-moulded commercial versions of our headsets, both wireless and F1 helmet, as well as get two contents finished to the highest standard, open a couple more studios and subvention our initial franchising plans.

"Can I ask you why you are looking for such a huge sum?" Michael asks James. "And what are you planning to do with it?"

James goes into an explanation the thread of which I lose a few times as it is about financial forecast, return on investments, exit strategy and initial investor returns.

I remember Michael querying why the initial investors would want to exit the company at this early stage. After a few more minutes of discussion, Michael finishes the conference call with, "Well, this is our offer. We wouldn't go any higher at this stage and if it's of interest, then let's proceed with the due diligence and make Vizuality a great success." James and Paul thank Michael and Eddy, confirm that they will be in touch and say their goodbyes.

I, personally, am in heaven. I can't quite believe what has just happened and although James' investment figure was high, I assume it was just a punt at trying to get as much as possible from the investors. At the risk of repeating myself, James has spent his entire life in investment banking, has been a trader and has led successful investments in the past. Since I know as much about Series A investment as

James knows about VR and tech, it seems to be a normal process.

As the conference call ends, the conversation with Michael and Eddy does not. We continue to discuss the company and they ask me further questions. Eventually after another 30 minutes, we shake hands and I leave the 25th floor with an, "I look forward to hearing from you" from Michael. We now need to confirm our acceptance of their offer and then initiate the due diligence process. Once the lift doors are closed, I can't help letting out a, "Come on!" with my clenched fist in the air!

As I come out onto California Street on a very pleasant blue-sky day, after a two hour and 40 minute meeting, I'm on a little cloud. Our company – our baby that we have worked so hard on for the past two years – is now pretty much on its way to becoming a big corporation. I grab a coffee at the Starbucks next door and start walking down the street. I'm going to grab a taxi back, but I need some time to reflect.

Since the title of this book clearly says that we did not make it past the end of 2016, it will come as no surprise that this offer of investment did not go through. However, this was not because of a failed due diligence or some retraction from Oppenheimer. Oh no. It did not even get that far.

I decide to take the train back, but the station where my Caltrain is going to take me to Palo Alto is nearly five miles across town. As I am slowly walking down California Street to grab a taxi to get me to the station, I get a call from James. I am expecting it as he told before the meeting that he would call me after it.

I am expecting to hear scream of joy at the other end with Paul and James cheering, but, instead, I get an angry voice from James saying,

"What a waste of time this meeting was. Who do those clowns think they are? It is a f'ing joke to offer that kind of money! I'm not here to play small change!"

With a few short phrases, I try to understand James' reasoning, but he is not even listening to me. It ends on an, ". . . our shareholders are not here for that kind of investment., They can put in that money themselves if they want. Let's discuss further on our return. See you back home. Bye."

Since Stan and I are flying back the next day and James and Paul are also flying back the next day but from a different airport, we are not going to see each other until about three days later when we are all back in our studio.

My little cloud of happiness has instantly disappeared, and it is completely deflated that I take the train back to our hotel in Palo Alto.

During the journey, I replay that meeting in my head again and again and can't stop thinking about how well it went and why in the world we wouldn't accept that kind of offer. Our closest competitor has recently received a similar sized investment, so it sounds like the way forward.

A few days later when we are back at base, we have our catch-up board meeting and the subject is brought to the table. I had a chance to discuss this in detail with Paul prior to the meeting and he obviously thinks exactly like me – he too can't understand why we are turning our nose up at this offer. James has not changed his tune: this is not a high enough investment. He has already discussed this with our shareholders and they agree that it is not worth it.

Unknown to us at the time, this was our last possible chance to save the company. From now on, it is doomed to fail. Not only because of the continuous spending frenzy, but also because of the recent events in Los Angeles as reported by Paul, the incomprehensible reaction from James with regards to the Oppenheimer offer and the fact that another US dollar credit card loaded with another £5,000 has been entirely spent. By now, Paul and I have lost pretty much all confidence in James and have even started to resent him. So much so that we start to etch a plan to try to salvage that investment offer behind James' back and, once sorted, to go and see our shareholders to put it to them. Yes, it is a risk, as if James has told us the truth and the shareholders agree with him that it is small change, then this will create even more problems. But somehow, we simply do not believe that James even mentioned the offer to the shareholders. Maybe it's a gut feeling, maybe we are getting used to James' feeble excuses.

Since the pitch deck mentioned to Eddy and Michael that we had "left back home" never even existed, Paul and I decide to draft our first pitch deck, as requested by Oppenheimer.

I think we do a good job of it; it looks good and is clear. We also have the business plan prepared by James a couple of month ago. It's not a great document, but it's useful. That's all we have, so I send an email to Michael and Eddy with Paul copied in to confirm the document requested in attachment and to tell them to let us know what they need from us next.

A day goes by with no news from Oppenheimer, then another and another.
"That's strange," says Paul. "Send them another email to chase them up and make sure they received the first one?" I do this, but a few more days go by and still no response at all.

Out of desperation, we then send Michael a direct message via LinkedIn in case our emails are not reaching him, but, yet again, no response. After a couple of weeks, we have to accept that they are not going to respond and that the deal is definitely gone.

In 2018 I was recounting that event with one of my clients who used to be a branch manager in a well-known UK bank. He told me that an offer like that from Oppenheimer should have been accepted the same day. They were expecting a call back that very same day to confirm our acceptance.

"An investment offer from Oppenheimer, which is well known for being a leader in technology investment banking, is a big opportunity that not only brings money to the table but would have also opened dozens of doors for you. You don't make them wait and you don't hesitate. If you do, they're gone," were his words.

Oh well, at least we tried. Of course, we did not know at the time that even if we had accepted that offer we would have failed miserably at our due diligence process. But, as they say, "Ignorance is bliss."

MY FAVORITE QUOTE

"If people like you, they'll listen to you, but if they trust you, they'll do business with you."
Zig Ziglar – author, salesman and motivational speaker.

LESSON LEARNED:

This Oppenheimer meeting was without a doubt one of the craziest (in a nice way) meetings I've ever had. What came out of it is that Michael – the investment manager from one of the largest tech investment banks – not only listened to me for about two and a half hours, but made us a multimillion dollar offer of investment.

So, although nothing came out of it, I will keep a fond memory of that meeting for a long time. This was certainly a successful meeting from a personal point of view.

WHAT WOULD YOU HAVE DONE?

1. Would you have accepted the Oppenheimer offer immediately, without any hesitation?

2. Would you have tried to negotiate the offer in an attempt to get a little more – not the amount asked by James – but maybe up to five million?

3. Would you have done exactly what James did and refused the offer as not being big enough?

Or maybe you would have done it completely differently? If so, please share what you would have done online at 1b1m1y.com

You can also log in to that website to view what other people would have done

CHAPTER FOURTEEN

Board of directors, minority rule!

It is now the middle of May 2016. We have been back from the US for just over a week and the atmosphere among the three directors has degraded even further. This upcoming board meeting is not going to improve things.

We're in a board meeting discussing a number of things, among them is a dismayed me asking James what is that £45k invoice we have just received from our lawyer for the month of April.

"How in the world can we be charged so much in one month? Is the lawyer now an employee of the company? Is he working full-time for us?" I ask James. "Oh, stop being a fool," James tells me.

"These people charge £600 an hour and that is what you have to pay if you want a decent service."

Yes, OK. But that is £45k in *one* month. Even at £600 an hour, that is still 75 hours of lawyer work this past month alone. Since the invoice only says, "Service rendered," it is impossible to know what has been worked on over those 75 hours.

The truth is that I'm livid. Since we started this company, we've had lawyers bill after lawyers bill every month. So far, barely six month into the company, we have already spent nearly £90k on lawyer bills alone. Yes, £90k!

James is treating me like a kid who hasn't got a clue how the corporate world works,

"You must realise that these people are doing crucial work for the company and that without this lawyer we don't stand a chance of any investments. The company's legal stuff must be all above board."

Yes, I don't know how the corporate world works. James is for sure right on that, but it does not explain anything to me and, therefore, does not make me feel any better that we have spent so much on one lawyer. All I'm asking is for the charged work to be explained and justified to me. I'm struggling to just take it for granted that our lawyer has billed for 75 hours last month and the cost is £45k.

Ironically, I might not have been wrong. James may have put me back in my place by telling me that our lawyer's work was absolutely necessary. Yet, that very same lawyer's work which we spent so much money on (by the end of the year, our total lawyer bill alone would come to £137k) came back to haunt us. More appropriately, it came back to haunt our investors, who the work of those lawyers was designed to protect. I'll tell you more about this later.

Paul and I have now started to audio record every single board meeting. Yes, we have minutes taken by our company secretary, but this is not at every meeting. Anyway, the minutes essentially highlight the points discussed and actions agreed, but they do not make a note of every negative remark or the ever-frequent disagreements taking place between the directors. So, audio recording is great. I'm not sure what they can be used for, but Paul is not walking into any of those meetings without the audio recorder switched on nowadays.

Next on the agenda is the Liverpool studio, as the building works are now nearing completion.

Paul and I have not been involved much with it as, from the start, James led the way and it has continued like that for most of the building work. However, Paul and I are now due to go over next week to talk to the contractor's electrical team, assess the various networking and electrical wiring requirements and prepare the final list of equipment needed.

As we discuss a few of the studio's cosmetic details, such as the technical console location, staircase and a few other things, James pulls a catalogue out to show us a thick blue carpet he has found. The studio flooring has already been laid in wood laminates, but James would like to cover the 72 square metres (775 square feet) of the studio area with this heavy blue carpet and have our logo emblazoned in the middle of it.

"Yes, it looks good. How much is it?" Paul asks.

"It's £10,000," responds James without batting an eyelid.

"£10k?" Paul and I question in unison. "Well, considering there is already a brand-new wooden floor as part of the refurbishment and considering the price, it can wait for later," we say.

"Too late!" says James. "I've already ordered it!"

Paul and I are flabbergasted. I mean, we are well used to James getting his own way, but this is blatantly being disrespectful to us as directors. We have not only not been asked, but we clearly disagree, yet it is shoved down our throats that we are going to have that £10k piece of carpet whether we like it or not and whether we agree with it or not!

Oh, and it doesn't stop there. During one of our other weekly meetings a few days later, we end up discussing the furniture for the Liverpool studio. James is showing us an antique mahogany-style furniture suite which he has chosen.

Personally, I think it is horrible and will not fit in a modern studio. I'm a minimalist and modern-style person and, considering that our VR studio is very much a futuristic product, I don't see how this old-style wooden furniture is going to fit in. Paul is in agreement with me, and as we open Google to start searching for something we feel is more suitable, it happens again. James throws his toys out of his pram once more and tells us to drop it, get on with our technology work and let him sort this out. He has made his decision: we are going to have the mahogany furniture and that is that.

We end the meeting on that note and I simply walk out of the boardroom without even a goodbye. I'm starting to have had enough of this nonsense attitude and of James treating us like his subordinates. He is already having his way with Stan who is jumping to his every beck and call, but I am not prepared to accept that attitude with us – the co-directors and founders of the company.

I walk out without saying anything I may regret. I consider myself a reasonably diplomatic person and, in any situation that degenerates, I will look for a way to resolve it peacefully and professionally. This time I am planning to do that.

How would you have felt if you had been in my shoes having to deal with this attitude? Do you think this is bad? Just wait. You haven't seen anything yet . . .

Paul and I have arrived in Liverpool. It has been a few months since we were last here and we have been told the studio should now be near completion. As we step inside the studio, we understand better why James has chosen the mahogany furniture. Basically, the studio has a red brick wall on one side and a white wall on the other. It has a very high ceiling crisscrossed with visible structural wooden beams, a series of ugly Victorian-looking chandeliers hanging from the ceiling and, to finish it off, old sash windows everywhere.

"Argh!" I don't know what to say. This looks truly awful in my eyes and I am so disappointed.

My response must have made an impact on Paul as I recall while talking to him last year about something completely different, he remembered my reaction that day with a laugh.

I guess since we have not been involved with the Liverpool studio much, we have only got ourselves to blame. Having said that, though, Paul and I had already prepared some designs even before James' big investment came in.

Back in the summer of 2015, we had started looking at a local warehouse that fitted our VR studio perfectly. We prepared layout plans, designs and concepts and, although we never signed a lease as we were not able to negotiate the right terms with the landlord, we had pretty much established how we were hoping our first and future studios to look and feel.

The plan had always been to open an initial three studios and operate them successfully so we could then start franchising the concept. To do that, we knew we needed a very identifiable brand and style. Our concept was a warehouse-style modern looking studio with metal railings, sliding doors, sleek and minimalistic furniture and lots of LED lighting and screens everywhere.

Although the signing of that warehouse did not happen, we did lease another big one as our main studio, but having chosen not to open it to the public just yet, we did not do any work on it so our design concepts stayed on paper. James had seen those designs and concepts and knew what we liked, yet clearly chose to go his own way – something which will not come as a surprise by now I guess.

"Oh well, what can I do now?" I say. It's just so disheartening to think that we are going to open our first public studio and it does not look anything like we want. Paul and I feel like we do not have a connection with that studio. It's such a shame.

At the end of the day, this Liverpool studio project has mainly been James' baby (figuratively and officially, as I will tell you later.) Since Paul and I were not overly supportive of the idea initially, as the decision is made to proceed we have had very little input on it. James has essentially got Stan to sort out the development so far.

Anyway, we are here to do a job so let's get on with it. Over the two days Paul and I are here, we start with the upstairs floor by marking the 24 different locations for the network point where we will connect the cameras; the HDMI extensions for the spectators' screens; the console location where we need extra power sockets; and the network points for the wireless transmitters.

We then move downstairs. Next to the main entrance and the public toilets, we are going to have the reception desk and, opposite that, we are going to have sockets and connectivity for two work desks where we, or other developers, can come and produce content for the upstairs studio.

In the second part of the downstairs space, taking up the whole left-hand side, is going to be the full-scale F1 simulator. So, we plan for the 25-amp socket supply, the console connection and the spectator screens. One of the obvious problems is going to be bringing the motion platform in. The F1 chassis comes in several boxes so this is not too much of an issue, but the six-axis motion simulator is a 600kg one-piece of kit. Thankfully, a discussion with the contractor confirms that they can remove one of the very large sash windows and crane the simulator in that way, so all is fine.

Before leaving, we also spot another issue that has not been planned for. The upstairs floor where the studio is located has 12 tall sash windows that have rounded tops. As we use optical tracking, the studio must be subject to minimal sunlight due to UV affecting the infrared tracking. We get the foreman over, discuss a way we can cover the windows and they agree that they will make 12 wooden covers for them. It's not ideal and it is not going to improve the studio's already odd aesthetic, but it should work fine.

After finalising everything with the electrical and building teams, we head back to the John Lennon airport to return to our studio. A few days later, we're due for another catch-up meeting and – guess what? – that meeting is going to be another "interesting" one!

Paul and I have prepared a detailed list of requirements based on our work in Liverpool. We need to go over the various items that need to be ordered, such as the optical tracking system made up of 20 cameras; two high-end computers so we can have two users at once in the studio; the networking systems; and the 3D prints and electronic components for our additional headsets.

As the new motion platform and full-scale F1 replica arrived a couple of weeks ago, they are currently stored with our shipper in Southampton waiting to be forwarded to Liverpool. We just need to sort out the smaller parts for it, such as the controllers, console and VR helmet.

As we sit down for our meeting, I refrain from bursting out my disappointment to James about the Liverpool studio look. At the end of the day, what is done is done. It's not going to change anything and would only add to our already tense relationship.

First, we start to discuss the upstairs studio. For the first time, we are going to do a topdown view installation, placing all cameras above the users. We then discuss where the tech console, spectator screens and mahogany furniture are going to be.

As for downstairs, we have measured up for the two developer desks, the F1 simulator and the . . .
"What F1?" interrupts James.

I look at Paul. Paul looks at me. I reply,
"Well . . . the F1 that is in Southampton that we purchased specifically for Liverpool."

"No, no, no," responds James. "It is not going to Liverpool anymore. There is a sound engineer studio underneath our studio and the wooden flooring will make too much noise as the simulator moves around. We can't put it there."

After a short moment of silence – my brain racing to work out whether I missed a board meeting at some point – I compose myself and then ask James,

"When did you plan to tell us? We never knew that! What are we going to do with the F1 platform and F1 chassis we have ordered?"

"I thought I told you," says James. ("Well, no, you didn't as usual," I strongly think to myself.)

"We'll keep the simulator and chassis in Southampton for the time being and we will use it in our next studio."

Well that is just great. So James went against Paul's preference of having one floor specifically because we could showcase the F1 simulator and a design studio downstairs, and now we're just going to have a couple of working desks and a reception in an area of about 100 square metres (1,050 square feet.) What a waste of space.

Aside from this "excellent" news, this once again pathetic meeting goes on to cover our next big event – our trip to Shanghai.

MY FAVORITE QUOTE

"Don't be cocky. Don't be flashy. There's always someone better than you."
Tony Hsieh – CEO of Zappos.

LESSON LEARNED:

Needless to say that, by now, my view of James is that of an egotistical person who likes to be "seen" and thoroughly enjoys having his bellboy Stan at his beck and call. James also very much likes to have his own way, clearly thinks that he knows better than anyone else and does not really like to take advice or ask permission.

The problem is that I have very little respect for this type of person. Not so much because they challenge me, but because the world is full of incredibly talented people. Some who save people's lives, some who solve critical situations, some who send astronauts into space and even some who resolve problems the majority of the world can't. Regardless of your skills and intelligence, however, we can all take advice from someone else at some point in our lives. It is the people who are open to other people's input who genuinely make the biggest difference of all.

WHAT WOULD YOU HAVE DONE?

1. Do you think that Paul and I have only ourselves to blame for the Liverpool studio situation for not being more "hands-on" on the development and progress and for not making a strong stand to James' decision of buying equipment and furniture without consulting us or against our decision?

2. Or do you think that James was totally out of order and abused his director's position but going ahead with purchases without consulting us or by deciding that the simulator was being pulled out of the studio without informing us?

Or maybe you would have done it completely differently? If so, please share what you would have done online at 1b1m1y.com

You can also log in to that website to view what other people would have done

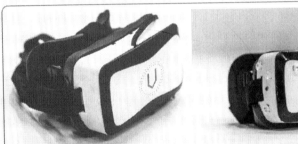

On the left, our very first prototype that we used at our events from January 2016 onward. On the right, that same headset upgraded with built-in LED for optimised tracking.

This is what untethered, large-scale Virtual Reality can do, single or multiple people walking, jumping, crouching and essentially freely exploring their VR world without any wires in the way. On the right, a visitor is testing our 64 square metres booth at the SVVR exhibition in San Jose - April 2016

Our 1.6 tons of equipments being loaded on the truck that is going to take it to California for our very first event in Los Angeles. This includes our F1 motion simulator and all the rigging we need for our booth.

On the left, the wireless receiver board with its cooling heat sink in grey and underneath it, the image processing board. On the right, the screen we were using with our headsets at the time.

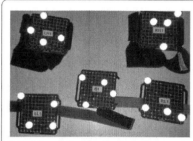 

On the left, a set of body tracking plates. They are made up of different patterns that the system recognises and are numbered accordingly (LL and RL for Left and Right Leg, LH and RH for Left and Right Hand and the B plate for the back. On the right, a couple of our Vicon tracking cameras we were using at the time.

Silicon Valley Virtual Reality Event (SVVR) entrance in San Jose at the end of April 2016. The place of many opportunities. At the SVVR, we started to use our new wireless transmission board, confirmed our partnership with BroadMesse, met our first client and got invited to discuss a $3 million investment offer.

On the right, the Liverpool studio as it was early 2016 when we first walked around the construction site. On the right, the opened studio as it looked once completed, including the expensive blue branded carpet.

On the right, the "near invisible" sign that points to the entrance of the studio. In the middle, our street signage and on the right, the large single letter signage located about 15 metres (45 feet) from the street.

The full replica chassis of our F1 simulator before painting. That was the simulator chassis due to be installed in Liverpool before the decision was made to keep it in storage. It ended up being sold for a fraction of its original price without ever being used.

On the booth at the Los Angeles Unity3D Vision Summit in February 2016. On the left, a visitor trying out our haunted house using the flashlight. On the right, our Unity3D sponsored F1 simulator.

The F1 simulator in our studio being developed and tested. The prototype VR helmet is a wired very high-resolution VR headset built inside a custom helmet (and eventually in a fully designed custom VR helmet). The black visor contains custom LEDs for head tracking performed by the optical tracking system mounted above.

A view of the content from an external (spectator) camera. The user in the simulator on the bottom left can see what the pilot in the car sees and is subject to every g-forces (simulated by our motion simulator) as if the user was really in that car.

On the left, our setup at the London Excel VRX event in March 2016. On the right, our booth at the Laval VR in rural France. The average VR area we had during our events was around 30 square metres (100 square foot)

On the left, this is the booth at the IAAPA Shanghai with our host BroadMesse. On the right, this is our booth at the IAAPA Barcelona in September 2016 with our host Attraktion.

Our booth at the SVVR in San Jose, in April 2016. The biggest booth of all!

On the left, some of the 3D CAD drawings of our commercial VR headset, on the right, the actual completed headset. It had IPD (Inter Pupillary) adjustment, independent focal adjustments, ejectable batteries on each side of the arms and was one of the very first headsets to have built-in headphones and to be fully wireless.

More people having fun with our technology and showing what wireless free-roam VR was capable of back then. On the right, the gentleman has crawled under a virtual table holding the flashlight in his hand. In the middle, the lady is hiding from the aliens attacking while on the right, the gentleman is very immersed in his fight against the hordes of aliens.

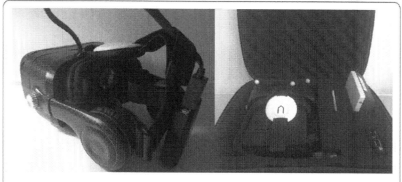

The second version of our commercial headset and the one supplied to our first client. The headset was based on similar designs as the previous one but improved to be slimmer and sleeker. On the right, the case it was supplied in to clients with the headset on the left, the transmitter on the top right and the battery on the bottom right.

1 Business, 1 Million, 1 Year

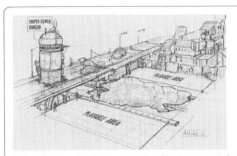

On the left, the drawing of the play area of our first client game. A 10 players free-roam wireless VR experience with 5 users in each playable areas. On the right, our 600 Kilos motion simulator arriving in the delivery bay of the hotel.

Screenshots of of some of our contents that I designed using Unity3D. On the right, our Moonbase where the user had to defend itself against invading aliens. In the middle, one of the very first VR experience I built showcasing five dinosaurs including the famous T-Rex. Finally on the right, an office space making use of the flashlight designed for a crime scene investigation style content.

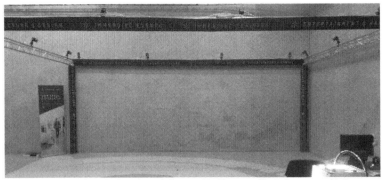

Our motion capture area for testing in our home studio covered by 16 cameras. The studio space was ideal as very large open space and high ceilings. It just needed a bit of cosmetic work to make it inviting to paying customers which we started to do toward the end of the year.

CHAPTER FIFTEEN

A royally messed-up opportunity

It is now the end of May 2016. While we have been away, our developer Frank and our simulation engineer Mikey have been progressing very well. The F1 simulator is looking good and working well. Of course, things can always be improved, but Frank is now working on developing the configuration interface and the game launcher. These are the remaining few things we have to do in order to have a commercially ready product. I am now really enjoying testing the simulator; it is fun and so realistic: after a 15-minute race my arms and neck hurt because of the simulated g-forces.

As for our VR studio, Paul and I have managed to put a lot of hours into it since returning from the US. Our latest improvement is the addition of hand and leg tracking.

By adding custom object markers strapped to the users' shoes and hands and working heavily on what is called "inverse kinematic" to replicate realistic body movements based on limited tracking points, we are able to track a full body naturally and have it interact with objects in the scene. One of our first tests is using our Alien Moon-based content with Paul on one side of the virtual sliding doors and me on the other. As the doors have a square window, we keep waving at each other on one side and then the other. The more recent improvements mean that we can now walk around one of our VR architectural kitchen contents and turn on the virtual cooker with our hands or push the virtual mugs and vases off the table. It's a lot of fun.

As you will recall, I mentioned Mr Dong visiting us in both Laval and San Jose and discussing in more detail with James the opportunity to distribute our technology in China. We have now signed a provisional agreement for his company to become the official distributor of our products in the whole of South East Asia and the Middle East, as they also have an office in Dubai.

To seal the deal and showcase our technology to their major clients, we are invited – all expenses paid – to Shanghai to attend the IAAPA (International Association of Amusement Parks and Attractions) which is held from 13th-16th of June at the SNIEC (Shanghai New International Expo Centre.)

This is one of three IAAPA events in the year and also one of the biggest. It covers thousands of square metres and has some of the biggest names in the attraction industry displaying there.

Since our host is also paying for our flights, they have sent us a proposed itinerary for the four of us (me, Paul, James and Stan.) Paul and I initially ask James why Stan is coming, as the three of us are more than sufficient to handle the event. James' response is,
"Stan is our head of sales and has to be there." We will not be doing sales, however, since our Chinese contact has explained to us that there will be a team of sales people from their company on the booth to handle inquiries – especially since many of them are likely to be in Mandarin!

However, there is an issue! Our host itinerary is proposing four return flights on Lufthansa in premium economy.
"There is no way we're travelling all the way to Shanghai in economy class!" shouts James once we've read the email with the flight details that has just arrived.

"Well, it's free and we're invited," I respond. "We can't be too picky!"

Paul tries to add his two cents, saying we're lucky to have such an opportunity and maybe we don't want to come across to our hosts as being too difficult, but that falls on deaf ears. James gets Stan to sort out business class flights with his contact who has been managing the flight booking. This will end up costing the company an extra £8,000 with our hosts paying the other half!

So here we are at Heathrow Terminal 5 once again. It is the 10th of June. This time, I am with Stan from London to Shanghai direct with British Airways, while Paul and James are going on Emirates Airways via Dubai. (Something to do with not all of us being on the same plane again in case of a crash!)

Although their flight was longer, they left a few hours before us, so James and Paul have arrived slightly ahead of us.

James and I have arrived in Shanghai Pudong Airport just after 5.30pm. We are greeted by Brian – the Anglicised name of the gentleman who is going to be one of our two hosts – and our driver for the week.
As soon as we're in the car, he drives us to a very posh restaurant where we are greeted by

our host and some of his Senior Management team. Paul and James are already here.

We're led to a private room where we are offered an amazing traditional Chinese dinner, complete with a huge round rotating table and small portions of various dishes being brought to the table one after the other. There are dozens of bowls of food to choose from. I'm exhausted, as it's been over 20 hours since we left home and I'm not sure what most of the dishes are, but I'm determined to return the hospitality of our hosts and respect their traditions. I try most of the food and end up having a pretty good dinner.

With the seven-hour time difference ahead of the UK, it is now 11pm and, after an amazing evening with our host, we are driven to our hotel – the Evergreen Laurel Hotel on Zuchongzhi Road. We are told by Brian that he will pick us up in the morning to drive us to the exhibition hall so we can start setting up the booth.

The following morning, Brian is there on time and we head to the SNIEC – which is only 10 minutes away on Fangdian Road. After getting our exhibitor passes and a rather long walk, we arrive at our host's booth which is where we will set up our studio under their brand. (See photos page 165.)

A team of half a dozen Chinese guys are there ready to help us set up and they have already put up the truss, saving us a couple of hours' work.

Our full setup is completed much quicker than usual and, once tested to make sure all is working well, we are ready to go. Later that afternoon, James lines up the plan for the next three days. Paul, Stan and I will be manning the booth while he will be sorting out the agreement with Mr Dong's team together with our respective lawyers.

This is a deal that can seriously change the company; it's not an investment, but a proper partnership. The broad lines that we have discussed with Mr Dong so far is that we are going to provide our entire solution and training as well as custom content for their clients and they will handle the sales, setting up and maintenance with us as a backup when needed.

BroadMesse is a leading exhibition company supplying to expositions, museums, showrooms, events and theme parks. With offices in Shanghai, Dubai and Germany, they also have clients in 80 different countries and count names such as Sony, Huawei and TP-Link among their customers. What an opportunity for us as such a young company!

It's the 13th of June 2016. The first day of the event goes well. Our host has lined up a number of clients to do a demo to and, with the huge amount of visitors as well, it ends up being a non-stop day of Paul, Stan and me relaying each other to run VR experiences with visitors while we talk to people and answer questions when not running the experiences.

It's an incredibly satisfactory day that we end with a meal and a couple of drinks at the pizza restaurant next door to the hotel. Come about 11pm, I've had enough and I'm off to bed as the next day is going to be another very busy one, so I'd better be rested. Paul follows me on his way to his room too, while we leave James and Stan at the bar.

It's 8.30am on the second day of the event. We've just had our breakfast and Brian is there ready to drive us to the exhibition centre as planned. Unfortunately, only Paul and I are there. We try to call James and Stan on their mobiles several times, but there are no answers. I even go back up to knock on Stan's door as his room is two doors down from mine, but after about 15 minutes we tell Brian,
"OK, let's go. I'm not sure where they are and we can't wait any longer."

As the show opens its doors, Paul and I are ready to handle the new flow of visitors, however, this time we end up running the booth by ourselves until 1pm when finally Stan decides to show his face.

"Oh, what a night it has been. Sorry I'm late, we didn't finish until 6am," a very tired looking Stan tells us.

Paul and I are livid. We – the two company directors – are there, ready and doing our job, yet our "head of sales" has come all the way to Shanghai to get pissed out of his brain and can't turn up in the morning.

It is not only completely disrespectful to me and Paul, but, more importantly, I am very well aware that we are on our host's booth and surrounded by many of their Sales team as well as our two hosts. This is not going to make a good impression. If someone was trying to mess up a deal, you couldn't do much better . . .

To top it all off, as Stan arrives at the booth, he kindly offers to get us lunch which we gladly accept. As he returns 20 minutes later with the three lunches, he is the first one to head straight to the meeting room, which we also use for staff breaks, to eat his lunch!

Paul storms into the room, throws Stan out and tells him to man the booth while he and I take our lunch first.

As for James, we did not see him at all that day. He did call us shortly after our lunch and told us that he was going to come over to the booth once he finished at the head office with Mr Dong, but we never saw him!

The third day goes well. Stan is there, but he is a slippery eel always wandering away from the booth for a cigarette or to talk to someone else making him unreliable to run the visitors' experiences.

We're getting tired. It's nearly the end of the fourth day of the event, we must have run our wireless VR experience with over 300 people by now and it is not slowing down.

We've had a number of meetings with some serious contacts. Our host has allowed us to talk to potential contacts that are outside the area covered by our distribution agreement, but they naturally want a record so if there are any deals made then we could negotiate a commission to them, which is fair.

So, over the last four days of the exhibition, we meet with one of the technical directors from Universal Studios; a representative of the newly-opened Disney Shanghai; and the director of the largest arcade in Dubai, who has already started to offer VR attractions and is extremely interested in opening one based on our technology. There is also an incredible opportunity to supply to a new US project consisting of around 200 40-foot trucks fully equipped with trailers that have mobile VR arcades fitted in them and which will be travelling around the US non-stop. The first pilot is ready to go, and they want to start with three lorries initially. They really like our product and concept. Finally, we have a team of three senior representatives come to see us three times over two days to talk about supplying some VR experiences to their Resorts World Genting – a Malaysian chain of luxury resorts and casinos which is expanding out of Asia.

During the last day, I take the opportunity to test out the experience offered by VRcade – the only other competitor offering a wireless VR arcade solution. We know it well by now, as some of the team tested our technology back at the SVVR. Their experience is quite different to what we offer. While their content is more advanced and polished than ours, it requires very little body movement, so the whole experience operates within a 3x3metre (10x10 foot) area.

It's good to check out what the competition is offering, and I am certainly jealous of their content is some ways because it is very polished. I'm not a big fan of the scores appearing on the screen when zombies are killed – for me, it kills the immersion. However, we have better and much larger tracking and make better use of our props. This makes me realise that we are going to need to improve our content a fair bit more.

The fourth day finishes a little earlier and we start dismantling the booth at around 3pm. With the help of about half a dozen of BroadMesse's staff, the whole thing is derigged and packed in less than two hours – brilliant! We definitely need to get a team to help us set up and derig our events in the near future, I think.

Meanwhile, James, together with our lawyer back home, has been discussing the agreement to draft the contract with BroadMesse's lawyers and to fine-tune the details.

We all meet back at the hotel and, as we are sitting in the lobby, James arrives back from BroadMesse' offices and throws the agreement onto the table in front of us.
"Well done guys. The agreement is signed. Let's make some serious money now!"

Finally, some good news. We really need that!

After a couple of hours to chill out and refresh ourselves, Brian is there to pick us up and take us out for dinner that we've once again been invited to by our host.

After a short drive to Shanghai's financial district, Brian parks the car and we join our host and some of his Management team along the banks of the Huangpu River. It's a short walk to the Paulaner Bräuhaus, a famous Bavarian restaurant. The atmosphere is great and everybody is in a party mood after this successful event and the signing of our agreement.

The next day, we have a little time off. Our return flight is not until later this afternoon, so we decide to go to the shopping mall across from the hotel as we want to buy a present for Brian – our host and driver – who has been formidable this week. He and his wife just had twin babies, so we want to buy a big toy for the kids and, as it happens, there is a Mothercare shop right across the road opposite the hotel.

This is the first time we actually get a chance to venture out of the hotel by ourselves, and the crossing of the six-lane Zuchongzhi Road is a scary moment.

There are traffic lights and pedestrian crossings, but that does not serve much purpose, as cars and a huge number of mopeds push their way across the crowd of crossing pedestrians to continue on their way anyway. Safety in numbers applies here, so we mingle in the middle of the large crowd of pedestrians and follow the flow.

That afternoon, Paul and I head into Shanghai city centre. We have very little time to explore, but one thing that really impresses me about Shanghai is that, for one of the largest cities in the world – with around 25million people living there – it is one of the cleanest cities I have ever visited. It is so clean that you could eat your lunch on the floor in the middle of the high street!

I'm sure there are other parts of Shanghai that are not as clean or modern and nicely maintained, but we did not have time to explore everything so I will keep my memories of the nice clean areas.

So, if this trip to Shanghai and the four-day event has been such a success, why did I name this chapter "A royally messed-up opportunity," you might be asking.

Quite simply because the entire trip, the extra money spent flying business class, the insane amount of work we put in this week and the absolutely incredible opportunities that could have come out of such a deal have all been wiped out by a pathetic agreement that has already been signed by both parties!

As incredible and eye-popping as it may sound, James and our lawyer, together with Mr Dong and his Legal team, have somehow managed to agree on a deal where we will supply the wireless headsets, the technology know-how and the content. However, considering that Vicon Systems – our motion tracking manufacturer – does not have a supply in China, the equipment we would supply would not only be expensive compared to local hardware but would also be subject to heavy Chinese import duty. If I recall correctly, it is about 30% on foreign-made hardware. Therefore, the agreement has a clause stating they will use a Chinese-made tracking system instead of ours!

As usual, James has made that decision without informing or consulting me or Paul before going ahead and signing the agreement. I did briefly browse it, but considering it's a lawyer-worded multipage document, I fell asleep after reading the first two pages of it on my return flight. In my defence, I had no reason to think that the agreement would be problematic or have such a deal breaker clause in it.

We have only been back home at our studio for a few days and there are already enquiries coming over from Brian and the team in China. They want quotes and advice on content development and, since neither Paul or I are yet aware of the Chinese tracking system clause in the agreement, we sit down, discuss the various requests and prepare quotes.

It is exciting. Finally we are in a position to start selling our products. We are in the process of finalising our headset designs to go for injection moulding so, once this is done in about three months' time, we will be able to deliver our products.

The quotation requests from Brian and the team back in China range from a small VR event with a single user due to cross a real bridge in a snow storm that costs around £80k to another one for a four-user 60 square metre (645 square feet) VR arcade showcasing Aido Wedo the mythical Chinese Rainbow Dragon. That one costs around £200k.

There is also a more standard entertainment setup for a large shopping mall that – if successful – will be deployed across their other shopping malls in China. Finally, there is one for a theme park that wants a brand-new VR attraction. They have a space of over 200 square metres (2,200 square feet) and want some custom content with a fast turnaround. This will be a huge development and, while we are unable to quote just yet as there are so many elements to it requiring clarification, we already know that this is going to be a £750k+ project.

However, as the quotes are finalised and sent over to Brian and the team, they come back to us informing us of the mistake we've made by including the tracking system. They would like us to revise the quotations without it. Paul and I are stunned.

"What does this mean? We can't supply our system without a tracking system. It won't work. What is going on?"

We meet up with James and Stan to report back on the quotation feedback. This is when we finally find out the intrinsic details of the signed agreement between James and Mr Dong that specifies they will source a China-based tracking system.

I don't know what to say. It's starting to be too many times that I'm completely taken by surprise.

"James, do you know how long it has taken us to get this tracking system working perfectly with our technology?" I ask. "And it's not only the tracking. It's also the various scripts we have written to provide integration with our solution to correct headset drift, for the props to be detected, for the virtual switches to work, for the multiusers to see each other, for the hands and feet tracking that we have spent a lot of time recently to make look realistic. This is hundreds and hundreds of hours of work!"

Paul also adds,

"We have even developed our own active marker LED tracking to improve the tracking." (Vicon only offers a passive solution of reflective markers) "And this, too, is a custom technology that would be difficult to adapt to another tracking system as it uses a very specific LED frequency to be recognised by the cameras."

For clarification purposes, at the time – the middle of 2016 – there are a very limited number of companies in the world that are capable of providing a reliable, accurate and very low latency optical tracking system. As a matter of fact, the number at the time that we are aware of is three! Of course, there are other smaller providers or even custom and open source solutions, but we tried some of them in the past and assessed that the tracking isn't always precise enough or it's jittery or has too much latency. While those systems may work for many purposes, for our VR project we need millimetre accuracy, sub-millimetres stability and ultra-low latency.

Additionally, one of the noticeable issues with other optical tracking systems is that as the number of objects tracked increases, so does the latency and, in many cases, other systems even limit the maximum number of tracked objects.

As we are now intending to track hands and feet, this requires us to track seven objects for each player (headset, prop, back and the four limbs.) As we are now testing four users at the same time, that is at the very minimum 28 objects tracked plus any additional external objects or props around the content that can be interacted with. We have tested our system with 50 objects so far without any noticeable latency drops, so we know that we can handle up to six users at the same time within the same tracked area if needed!

As you can imagine, I am sitting there completely haggard, looking at Paul, and Paul looking at me. We are both completely speechless! I simply have no words as do not know what to say or where to start. I could cry!

However, luckily for us, James is his usual assertive self,
"Well, I'm sure it can be worked out. They can develop the tracking on their side and we can provide them with the wireless headset and know-how."

"But how are they going to develop the tracking?" I ask. "They want to supply their client. There has never been any talk of them having to provide a team to develop a tracking system made in China. We don't even know if there is a decent optical tracking system available in China and, if there is, whether it works properly!"

I can see the deal slipping away from us just like that. I can't believe that, once again, a decision has been made by James without consulting us. This has turned out to be a royal fiasco. I am seriously thinking of calling an EGM and putting it down to the shareholders to make a decision: "You choose. It is me or James, but I can't continue working like this."

To be perfectly honest, this was so impossibly bad that, at the time, I even wondered if it was a hidden camera show and whether a camera crew was going to burst into the room with James laughing at me. But sadly, no. It was all too real.

Over the following few weeks, we try to salvage the deal by providing lower cost packages cutting our margins.

We talk to Brian explaining the situation and he does send us some Chinese tracking system details that he thinks may be suitable. We explain to him that even if we find a suitable tracking system, we have limited resources to work on and it will take us months to get a properly tested tracking system to work with our headset and content. Even if we manage this, we cannot guarantee that it will work well at this stage, so it is dangerous to confirm any quotes.

Despite the fact that a week after returning from China we have a major press release announcing the partnership to the world, published by the majority of the tech press, the emails from Brian and the team become more sparse. Within a couple of months we have pretty much lost contact with them and nothing comes from our Chinese agreement.

Failing to accept the investment offer from Oppenheimer was seriously bad, but how about this one? This should rate as the mother of all failures, surely?

MY FAVORITE QUOTE

"There are no secrets to success. It is the result of preparation, hard work and learning from failure."
Colin Powell – US statesman and retired four-star General in the United States Army.

LESSON LEARNED:

I don't think I need to explain to you why I chose this quote from Mr Powell. It describes James' attitude to business in three clear and concise expressions. "Preparation, hard work and learning from failure" is quite clearly something James does not do. This, unsurprisingly, results in the most miserable of failures.

WHAT WOULD YOU HAVE DONE?

1. Would you have involved yourself with the negotiations and made sure the entire agreement was sound before allowing it to be signed?

2. Would you have allocated all resources to find a suitable Chinese tracking system and worked hard over the following few months to develop the integration and get it working with our system, even with no guarantees that we could get it to work?

Or maybe you would have done it completely differently? If so, please share what you would have done online at 1b1m1y.com

You can also log in to that website to view what other people would have done

CHAPTER SIXTEEN

Space agency technology

It's now the end of June. We've only been back from Shanghai for ten days and Paul and I are heading to Toulouse in the south of France for a meeting at the CNES (National Centre for Space Studies.)

At the Laval Virtual event at the end of March, we met with a gentleman named Francois who acts on behalf of the CNES' interests. They believe they have developed a tracking technology being used for the ISS (International Space Station) that could work for us and would like to discuss potential licensing.

The party we are meeting is made up of JP, the patent owner and inventor of the technology; Michel, a super bright physicist who uses the technology in practical applications for the CNES missions; Francois, our contact who has organised the meeting; and Bernard, one of the project directors.

They proceed to explain to us that the technology was invented and refined over many years to allow astronauts on EVAs (Extravehicular Activities,) also known as space walks, to allow them to precisely locate a specific area of the ISS needing maintenance. The technology is based on a custom designed microchip that, aside from returning orientation information, provides very accurate magnetic field calculations.

Without getting too technical, the devices are able to precisely measure the magnetic field of a room and, once calibrated, "know" where each of the devices are in that room in relation to the zero point. So, to a certain extent, this is similar to our optical tracking system with the major exception that there are no cameras needed for this.

After a long discussion on the technology and what they would like to get out of the negotiations, they take us into a large meeting room. In the room, there is a laptop placed on a small round table, a projector displaying the laptop screen on a wall and a few chairs for us all to sit on.

They also have one of their devices connected via a USB cable to the laptop currently resting on the floor. The engineer explains to us that they have previously calibrated the room and we are now seeing on the screen their MATLAB software showing the magnetic field measurement that the devices pick up.

The engineer then picks up the device and starts moving it around. The graph display on the screen changes as the magnetic measurement changes depending on where the device is. As it is placed on the table next to the laptop, the graph display stops at a specific value which the engineer makes note of for all of us to remember later.

He then moves the device to a new location at Paul's feet and, again, makes a note of the graph values. Finally, he returns the device to its original zero point and shows us how the graph has returned to zero. Then again, he moves it to the first location and shows us how the graph now shows the same values as the first time. Finally, he moves the device back to Paul's feet and shows us how the graph shows the same values as the second position from the last time round.

This may sound boring to most people, but Paul and I are in awe. What we have just witnessed is a single device that is capable of reporting its exact position in a calibrated location without relying on any external cameras or devices. If we can adapt this to work with our headset, this would remove the need for an optical tracking system. It would also mean we would be able to add a joint patent to our company's intellectual properties.

Of course, it is not that straightforward. The device will need some serious algorithm work to translate the magnetic field measurement into a six-degree position and it will also need a wireless connection to transmit the data back to the PC as, at the moment, the device is wired only. But that's not impossible, just more hard work. We are pretty used to that anyway!

We're staying in a small hotel in the centre of Toulouse as we have taken this opportunity to meet up with a French company based there that has developed a 3D face scanning booth. We are intending to offer this to allow our users to scan their faces before starting a game and have their real 3D face mapped to their VR avatar.

Before returning home, we are invited by the CNES team to a celebration evening at the City of Space in Toulouse. Our collaboration is all agreed in principle, but tonight at the event we will be meeting with their main negotiator to discuss the general terms of a potential agreement. We have been assured that they are not talking to anybody else from this type of industry with regards to this technology.

The next day we fly back home in time for a board meeting where we review and discuss the huge potential that this tracking technology has for our company. We all agree that we need to get this agreement signed as soon as possible.

During that board meeting, we also review the F1 simulator. This is now looking good. We are having to make small adjustments to the platform and weight balance, as there are some annoying vibrations, but for now the progress is excellent. We are also discussing with our 3D designers the commercial version of our VR helmet. As it stands, we believe the F1 simulator will be ready for sale in three to four months from now.

During that meeting, we review the progress of our university agreements. Portsmouth is keen to get things moving forward. During a recent trip there, we identified a suitable site by the docks which could become our second public VR studio, but would also be used by the university for research and development.

We will need at least £25k to get it going, but there is a possible government grant to apply for, since this is partly for education. We need to look at an application.

Everything seems to be happening at the same time. All the seeds that we have planted in the last few months are starting to blossom and it makes for a very busy couple of weeks. We have a new quotation that has come in for an Australia-based company we met back in Shanghai. This is a huge requirement for a theme park from a verified and established source. They would like a VR attraction to cover around 900 square metres (nearly 10,000 square feet) – a project that will be worth in excess of a £1million.

We have also been contacted by Jack M From General Motors in the US. We don't recall him much, but we met him at an event in the US, he is a project director at the huge General Motors company and he would like to meet with us to discuss potential synergies. The concept he wants is for people to be able to walk around their vehicles, but we're not sure yet if they are talking to use from a design aspect or from a sales aspect.

We are also in discussion with Anthony from VR Sports who is planning to open a series of sports-based VR arcades and seems to have excellent credentials and connections.

There is also Mysterious Ways, a company looking to offer a touring nine-week VR show to people in the UK. They need our technology for their show.

We are talking to CKAS, the supplier of our motion platform in Australia, who seem keen to open a VR arcade in Melbourne. Finally, we are in discussions with Enterspace – a Swedish company with connections in the UK that is looking to open VR pods for museums.

In total, we have over 25 quotations in the pipeline for various projects ranging from £80k to over £1million.

Last but not least, there is also Igor and his team in Indonesia who we met at the SVVR six weeks ago. We are now in very advanced talks with them. They are an animation studio that has produced several TV animations in Indonesia. They have developed their own VR content and we are now working with them to customise it to make it work with our technology.

Their VR arena concept is two areas that are 15 metres long by five metres wide (45 feetx15 feet) running side by side. Each of the areas is individually tracked with five people in a team playing against each other.

The VR content makes full use of the large areas that are separated in the middle by a VR crevasse. Each of the teams has a tower that a player can climb to have a top-down shooting position on the other team.

Once their first arcade is opened in Jakarta, they plan to expand rapidly across south east Asia by opening franchised concepts. The overall project is going to cost around £200k, but they are going to start with a reduced version using two vs two players. We have given them an initial quote that is just over £50k.

MY FAVORITE QUOTE

"Opportunities don't happen. You create them."
Chris Grosser – photographer and businessman.

LESSON LEARNED:

That is certainly a very true quote. The opportunities described in this chapter are only a few of the best ones we've had recently.

Between all of them, we have quotations in 11 different countries, some seriously exciting developments bringing large potential revenue to the company.

This is deserved, as we have worked very hard over the last few months to improve and showcase our technology. I can't help but wonder, however, if we would have had all of those opportunities if we hadn't spent the kind of money James has made us spend on sponsorships, attending large events with our full kit, our expensive branding process, etc. Maybe it was money well spent after all?

WHAT WOULD YOU HAVE DONE?

1. Do you think James was right to spend all that money on showing ourselves off at the international events? If we hadn't done this, would we not have had as many opportunities?

2. Do you think those opportunities would have happened even if we had spent a lot less money, if we had been at events without sponsoring them or having the biggest booth around?

Or maybe you think completely differently? If so, please share what you would have done online at 1b1m1y.com

You can also log in to that website to view what other people would have done

CHAPTER SEVENTEEN

The Grand Opening

As the finer details of the BroadMesse agreement become clearer, it obviously increases the already high tension between me and Paul on one side and James on the other. Thankfully, all the recent opportunities and the huge potential of the CNES technology have softened the mood a little.

The working relationship between the three directors is not healthy for the company and we know that very well, so we are trying very hard to be diplomatic and make things better. Quite clearly, James has the full trust of the investors as our third funding instalment has recently been paid into our bank account. This is another £240k.

We have now received over £1million in funding – £1,080,000 to be precise – and we are now eight months into the business since the investment was officially signed. While we have tremendous business opportunities, the fact that we have been spending money at an average rate of £100k a month is quite daunting.

Having been in business myself for a while, I'm very aware that many start-ups fail within their first year of operation. I'm also aware that there is a general view that – unless you're the exception to the rule – most start-ups rarely break even until their second or even third year of operation. Since we've had this opportunity of a huge investment, I am keen to make it last long enough for us to be profitable and sustainable, but this has not been the case so far!

As much as the additional loan note was a formality, it has come with a warning from the shareholders that the company must start to bring revenue in. The additional £500,000 funding offered initially, which is yet to be released, was to take the company to the next level, not to keep funding its extravagant lifestyle while it attempts to bring a product to the market. This is a warning that unless things drastically improve saleswise, we are at risk of not receiving any further funding. With hindsight, I would agree with this entirely.

Since you might be wondering, let me break down how we have spent over £800,000 in eight months so far:

- There was an initial £50,000 to buy back the shareholding from the previous investor.

- Over £120,000 has been spent on lawyer fees and services, essentially to produce employment contracts, company structuration, shareholder agreements, director agreements, the BroadMesse agreement and registration and patent applications.

- Just under £30,000 so far in accountancy fees and services. This was to form our five initial companies, complete the annual returns and provide secretarial services.

- Over £80,000 in travel and entertainment that includes hotels, flights, meals and drinks! That sounds a lot on the surface, but when we consider that our first trip to LA back in February cost us nearly £25,000 between all business class flights and the hotel, the costs mount rapidly.

- Attendance and sponsoring of the events have added another £115,000 to the cost.

All those events are generally sold by the square metre (or square foot) of booth space and, since we've had some of the largest booths at recent exhibitions, it is easy to see how the costs can climb quickly too. Being a Platinum sponsor of the SVVR event in San Jose back in April, cost us £40,000 to attend. Then there are the extras to pay, such as electricity, signage, insurance, etc.

- And, of course, to attend those events we need to have our equipment with us. This is about 500kg of stuff to carry across several flight cases and crates for the VR studio alone, and about 1,600kg (1.6 tons) for when we took the F1 simulator with us. To carry this, it has cost us nearly £45,000 in shipping as well as some storage fees for when the equipment was in transit or for storing our F1 and simulator after arrival.

- There was also the branding back in December and January. For a brand-new identity, a website, brochures and a video, the total cost was nearly £60,000.

- The company wage bill is now around £16,000 a month and has so far cost us nearly £80,000 since the start of the year.

- A crucial element to getting our headsets commercially ready means we had to get 3D CAD drawings done by a designer and samples printed, as well as getting the finished headset parts 3D printed professionally at a cost of nearly £20,000.

- The preparation of the Liverpool studio has cost us a little on signage, extra carpet, some customisation on the stairs and getting the window shutters done. So far, this has come to about £30,000, although we have just purchased and received around £60,000 of hardware for it which is due to be paid for by the end of the month.

- Finally, we have spent the remaining £140,000 on hardware and overheads, including a 24-camera tracking system, four top-of-the-range computers, two motion simulator platforms and two F1 replica chassis, as well as office computers, headset components, exhibition booth equipment, props, insurance, electricity rates, fees, etc.

- The remaining is what we have left on our business account which – with the last instalment paid – brings this to around £280,000.

It doesn't take a genius to work out that, on the list above, the only realistic value for the company are the assets. The remainder has gone into events, fees and trips.

However – as mentioned before – the extravagant spending on sponsoring events and marketing us as the company to watch has actually been beneficial. It has not only raised the attention of investors, but has helped us secure some amazing agreements and deals so far.

It is Tuesday the 5th of July 2016. Paul and I are flying once more to Liverpool to spend three days installing the tracking system and console and preparing everything for the planned opening in ten days on the 14th of July.

As we arrive in Liverpool, we discover the new signage that has been installed recently. This is made up of a large illuminated portrait sign with a large "V" on it (for the initial letter of the company) that is placed on the external wall of the top floor. Although it is visible from the street which is about 15 metres (45 feet) away, it is not obvious at all what this is about.

Considering that our main company logo is a landscape format with the full company name, we can't help but wonder why this shortened version has been chosen, as it does not say anything to passers-by. As we walk around to the main entrance, there is also a sign by the stairs leading to it: a clear perspex square with the company name and logo on it.

It would look fine other than the fact that the sign is attached to a red brick wall and, since whoever decided to use that logo chose a multicoloured one, it is literally invisible over the red bricks unless you are right next to it. (See photos page 165.)

We then walk up the stairs and step inside the studio. The ground floor is a long, 100 square metre room with a couple of toilets and a small meeting room on the left. The remainder of the floor is occupied by a single chunky mahogany desk that is due to act as a reception.

There is nothing else in that room, so it is a little echoey as we walk in and talk to each other! Also on that floor, James has got some colour-changing LEDs installed which are supposed to light up the wall. We were not very keen on them initially, but James said that he got them at the discounted price of £3,000 for 12 of them – although that was James' figure. The real one, the one that we got invoiced, for was £4,800! Yes £4,800 for 12 LED lights and installation.

Admittedly, they are nice and light up the wall above each of the LEDs. The colour-changing effect is quite efficient . . . at night.

You see, the problem is that those lights are completely ineffective during daylight, as they are not powerful enough to be visible in a studio that has 10 very large windows with no shutters on them. Since the studio is due to be used mainly during the day, the money spent on those lights would end up as being completely wasted.

As I discovered those additional low points in the Liverpool studio, it made me feel even worse about it than I did already. I believe that, as a company, opening up your first public venue should be an exciting time and a moment to be very proud of, but since the entire Liverpool studio from design to finishing touches has been out of our control and on the rare occasions when we tried to be involved, we got told to basically mind our tech duties, I just cannot feel anything for it and I think it is such a shame.

So right now, I am standing in our first public venue due to be opened in 10 days' time, and I do not like the decor or furniture used in it. I do not like the fact that it is over two floors with an unused one. I don't really like the look of the wooden shutters that have been built upstairs to cover the sunlight. I don't like the signage, and I don't like the price list that James has produced.

You see, the price list – like so many other things related to the Liverpool studio – has also been the subject of a disagreement in our last board meeting. James got the price list printed without consulting us (obviously!) so Paul and I have only found out recently that the cost to use our Liverpool studio is going to be £300 an hour!

When Paul and I are told, we nearly fall off our seats.

"Who is going to pay that? That's very expensive!" says Paul.

"And what about the gamers and developers? They're not going to pay that! And what about when there are one or two people who want to use the studio for a 20-minute game, for example? Are we going to do a pro-rata tariff?" I ask.

If I recall correctly, this is where one of James' famous phrase started to appear,

"I don't want spotty teenagers playing games and wrecking my studio!" James replies. "This is a professional studio and, as such, the price is relevant."

James' idea is that the studio is solely going to be used for professional purposes such as architects showing their plans in VR to their clients, large projects that need VR visualisation being developed, commercial VR training, and so on.

While Paul and I do not disagree that VR is incredibly powerful for architectural visualisation, as this was one of our key presentations when we launched back in June

2015, we can't see this type of demand keeping the studio sufficiently busy enough. We had in mind that, during the day, the studio would be a professional VR offering on a reservation basis – although we had a more reasonable £120 per hour price tag in mind. From 6pm every evening, as well as weekends all day, the studio would then open its doors and operate at least one of our completed VR content (with more to be released as development progressed) to the general public, birthday parties and corporate events.

"No way!" says James. "No gaming in the studio!"

As for the tariff card, James tells us that,
"It is easier to reduce the price than increase it if you start too low."
That is an odd way of seeing things as, in my view, if you start with a low tariff card and are very busy, then you increase the prices. Yes, some people may be annoyed, but it is called "supply and demand."
If, however, you start with a high tariff card and reduce it because you have overpriced yourself and are low on attendance, then you are saying to your clients that you are not selling enough so you can get a discount. Well, that's my view anyway!

As you can see now, this Liverpool studio is as opposite of an idea of a VR studio that I was hoping for, hence my total dislike for it at this stage. But, I am professional and I am diplomatic. It is a company-first studio and, regardless of my views and feelings, I will go along with what James wants and I will do the best I can to make sure this Liverpool studio works and becomes popular.

After five days back at base, we have again returned to Liverpool, this time for the official launch on the 14th of July.

We've arrived the day before to check that everything we set up the previous week is up and running and that everything is working correctly. With a size of 12m long x 6m wide (40 feetx20 feet,) the tracked area of our new VR studio is occupying two-thirds of the first floor. At the far end, there is a spectator corner with the old furniture and a large TV screen. On the opposite end, we have our management console where our computers, server and tracking equipment is located. We have strategically placed our wireless transmitters across the studio for good coverage and we have our three main contents on display and working very well. (See photos page 163.)

D-Day is here and everything is ready for the grand opening. This morning at breakfast, James is eating at the table with a couple of our shareholders who have come over for the opening while Paul, Stan, a couple of our staff and I are on the table next to them. When James finishes his breakfast, he gets up and, as he walks past our table, he calls his bellboy,

"Stan. Now."

On those two words, Stan – who is in the middle of eating his scrambled eggs – drops his spoon and napkin, gets up and walks out straight after James, his mouth still chewing the rest of his breakfast. We cannot help looking at each other and bursting into laughter as it is so pathetic. This has been James and Stan's rigmarole for a while now.

James has planned "his" opening party very carefully: expensive canapés, champagne and drinks at a cost of £4,000. Invites have gone out to all our contacts in recent months, as well as the press and selected specialised magazines. The result is an attendance of about 50 people throughout the whole day.

Yes, I did write correctly: only 50 – as in the numbers five and zero – people turn up! Oh, and out of those 50 people, a dozen of them are staff, shareholders and family, another six are our colleagues from the development studio next door, we have a few people who have accepted the invite to try out the studio and then there are around a dozen press people. To say that it is not very busy is an understatement, but Paul and I do the honours, we cut the red ribbon that James has prepared, we run the shows and get people to experience our studio – especially our newly improved Egyptian temple with reusable space and realistic flame torch.

At the end of the day, we close the studio, we all go for dinner and drinks to complete the celebration and return home the next day. This was the last time the studio would be open to the public! Yes, you read correctly: the Liverpool studio was closed on the same day as the opening day, never to open again. Crazy, you think. Yes, totally. You see, the problem is that James has not planned for anybody to man the studio when we aren't there. And as we are a two-hour flight away, it is not that straightforward for us to come over and open up for public sessions. James really expected that once the studio had been launched, the development guys next door would be using it on a daily basis with their clients and there would be a queue of architects and designers lining up outside waiting for their turn. It does not work like that, though, and obviously there was never a queue or even a single person waiting.

Stan, our "head of worldwide sales," is tasked by James to fill up the studio and get people in, but whatever his tactics are, he clearly is not successful. Paul and I returned to the studio about four times after that: once to train our colleagues next door on how to run the studio, use the kit and calibrate if necessary. It was all unnecessary, however, as they never made use of it. We also met some potential clients there, a museum, a design studio and a couple of guys who came from New Zealand to see our kitchen designs, but we only opened it privately, not to the public. As soon as the meeting was done, we shut the doors, turned the lights off and flew back home.

As heartbreaking as it is to say, the Liverpool studio didn't make a single pound of income, yet cost the company around £90k in total in building work, design, modifications, carpet, furniture, LED lights, marketing, launch event, tracking equipment, computer systems and initial rent. That's £90k flushed down the toilet, as well as a huge amount of time that could have been far better spent on other developments.

MY FAVORITE QUOTE

"I never dreamed about success, I worked for it."
Estée Lauder – founder of Estée Lauder cosmetics.

LESSON LEARNED:

This quote is interesting because most of us have dreams of success, of money or whatever else, but how many of us are actually prepared to work hard to achieve them? And when I say "work hard," I mean work beyond any natural or logical limits, like seven days a week, 16 hours a day and even when finally getting some "home time," still having to deal with calls, emails and text messages.

A friend once told me a phrase that I love: "There are many people who want a job, not many who want to work." I'm not sure if this was from him or if he read it somewhere, but it is so very true.

WHAT WOULD YOU HAVE DONE?

1. Would you have taken over the management of the Liverpool studio and insist on it being used as a general public / gaming studio in the evenings and weekends?

2. Would you have done what we did and let James run it the way he thought was right using a price list he thought was suitable but clearly was not?

Or maybe you think completely differently? If so, please share what you would have done online at 1b1m1y.com

You can also log in to that website to view what other people would have done

CHAPTER EIGHTEEN

Financial forecast clash

It's the Monday after returning from our "Grand Liverpool Opening" and we are preparing the agenda for a couple of board meetings. The first one is a small internal board meeting to discuss forecast and plan the minuted board meeting due to take place the following week to do with the status of the company, progress so far and plans for the months ahead. We have had to split the board meetings recently because there is so much to discuss and review that they can easily end up lasting four or more hours without covering everything needed. What is interesting is that in the space of the next 12 days, as tensions escalate and things came to a head, we end up having five board meetings. And if you wonder how I can recall those exact events nearly three years on, it is simply because

I have the meeting minutes and recordings on my next screen as I am typing this paragraph.

As previously mentioned, the relationship between the three directors has been deteriorating for weeks now, and the Liverpool opening fiasco has not helped to ease things off.

Coupled with the ongoing spending that does not seem to be slowing down, Paul and I are growing increasingly frustrated as we feel we barely have any control on the different events that are happening. I would like to say that there is good news on the horizon and the storms will be easing out, but sadly we are not even near the eye of the storm yet!

The first of the board meetings is just a catch up, so the three of us meet in our office's boardroom. Paul is recording the meeting and we initially start to discuss "how well the launch went." It is difficult to keep calm as, while sure enough the launch went really well, we have had very positive feedback so far, James got interviewed on ITV and we've had some really cool articles in the press, Paul and I are not exactly impressed at the number of attendees, or at the price list or at the non-existing prospects. We mention that and James reassures us that it is all in hand and that Stan is now actively following leads and organising bookings.

We then discuss a few other matters covering the CNES tracking system process as well as the various quotations that have been produced recently and, finally, we move on to discuss the financial forecast that James has prepared for the next six months.

James is technophobic. For those who do not know what that terms means: James is not really into technology or its usage. This is quite odd when you think that he is a director in a company that is involved with the latest technology trends!

Having said that, I am no financial person. I'm rather good at maths and as a software developer I do understand a lot of the number logics, but I have never been a fan of accountancy or forecasts, so I guess we all have our strengths and weaknesses. As James is the financial guy and Paul and I are the technical guys, we complete each other quite well. However, what happens in that meeting is rather unexpected!

Since James is not the most technical guy around, all his financial reviews and forecasts so far have always been on paper with numbers added by hand or on a calculator. As the tech guy, I'm not much in favour of that as I think that having a forecast on an Excel spreadsheet allows for easy manipulation and changes to see the results in real time. But it is what it is. James hands me and Paul a copy of the paper forecast that he has prepared for the company's next 12 months covering the period from August 2016 to July 2017.

We take a few long minutes to review it. Focusing all my attention on the coming months that take us to the end of the year, I soon realise that James has forecast us to receive an income of £180k and to have outgoings of £320k. I review this again and double-check everything, as things don't seem right.

I know I have mentioned it a few times before, but just want to repeat that I am a pretty cool-minded guy in general. I rarely, if ever, lose my temper; I rarely, if ever, let a stressful situation take the better of me; and I generally always try to find a diplomatic way to resolve conflicts or issues in any situation. So, I don't know what happens this time. I guess the accumulation of so many disappointments, the frustration at James for messing up so many opportunities recently, being extremely tired after the long months of hard work or maybe a combination of it all, but that forecast is just too much to take on and I blow out.

I start to shout at James that this is a ridiculous forecast. I ask him – without waiting for an answer – what would happen if we did not receive the forecasted £180k (as, yes we have lots of quotes and lots of interest, but, as of that day, no sales signed yet) and I ask him how he can still forecast a spending of over £65k a month considering that we currently have less than £280k in the business bank account with known liabilities over the next three months of nearly £100k. At this rate, we won't even last another four months and, again without waiting for an answer, I ask James how he is planning to go into 2017. Even if we did receive £180k revenues, by January we would be pretty much in the red anyway.

I tell him that the forecast he had produced is not worth the paper it is written on, that my young son could have produced something better and, to be perfectly honest, if we do not take drastic steps, our company will be closed by the end of the year. I storm out of the boardroom, smashing the door closed behind me to the astonishment of everyone else in the office. After that clash, James does not call me to discuss it, he does not come by the studio and we do not talk for another four days.

After I calm down, Paul and I have a meeting to discuss this and, as it does not take a genius to work out that the forecast was a total piece of trash, we take the very unusual steps to draw our own forecast that we are going to impose on the company as the two majority shareholders. I call it "The Vizuality Rescue Plan."

I am not the best person to draw up the forecast, but considering the now critical point that the board of directors has reached, a major change has to happen and we have very little time. We have another official board meeting the following week. I want this to be discussed and passed at that meeting so we can take immediate rescue actions and try to save the company.

I know deep down that we are in a critical position and I even tell my wife that if something does not drastically change, the company will be shut down by December!

I know it is going to take even more hard work to save the company now, but I am more determined than ever.

It's the 22nd of July 2016. Our official board meeting, minuted by our company secretary, starts with a financial review of the year. Needless to say, it is pretty bleak. James agrees that there has been a loss of control of the finances, but that he has the next loan facility agreement ready and it just needs to be approved by the shareholders. As far as Paul and I are concerned, it is good news to know that we have reserved funding, but we cannot and should not continue to haemorrhages money like we have in the past few months. We put our financial rescue plan forward to be discussed in great depth.

Our financial rescue plan is drastic. We have budgeted for a maximum spending of £17.5k a month for the next five months. This does not take into consideration any new loan facilities and is in order to make sure we end the year in a positive cash flow, even if we do not get a single sale by then.

Here are the 14 points copied from the Financial Rescue Plan that we put forward. I will expand on the reasons for them afterwards:

- Termination notice is to be given to the town office
- We need to sell the Mac computer
- We need to sell the car chassis and motion platform which are in storage in Southampton
- Our working studio needs to open to the public at weekends
- Change Stan to a zero-hour contract
- Cut down the directors' salaries by 20%
- All staff to accept a pay cut of 10% and cut down their hours by 10% per week
- No individual purchases above £20 on the directors' card. Anything over this to be approved by a purchase order to be signed by any two directors
- Travel expenses, hotels and restaurants to be limited to the strict minimum
- Meals while away to be restricted to £50 or below per head per day, including drinks
- Liverpool studio to be opened at weekends and evenings

- Maximum monthly expenses for lawyer, bank fees and accountants to be £500. If quote is more than this, to be approved in advance by two directors
- Notice be given to investors to request deferral of £2,400 monthly interest payment
- No further money to be spent on the Liverpool studio, unless agreed in advance by any two directors and completion of a purchase order

The first point is going to save us £500 a month. This is because when we initially moved to our main studio, James decided to rent out a small office in town for Stan and him to work from, as they did not like working from the studio. Yes, I agree that the studio has no windows and is a bit cold and empty looking, but we have a good deal there. Paul, Frank, Mikey and I have been working from there, so it is a bit of a waste of money to have a second office space when we have plenty available at the studio.

The sale of the Mac computer is going to bring in £2,000. The Mac Pro was initially purchased alongside a giant screen at James' request, but we never really made proper use of it so it was stored in the town office. Any other standard Windows computer would serve an equal purpose.

The car chassis and the motion simulator cost us £60k and have been stored in Southampton for nearly three months now, still in their packaging. If we can sell them – even at a slight loss –this could add £45k or thereabouts to our account.

We then estimate that by opening our working studio to the public every weekend, we can generate between £4,000 and £6,000 a month. We need to spend around £5,000 to do some cosmetic changes to the studio to make it more welcoming, but otherwise it is ready to accept paying customers.

We also propose to change Stan's contract to a zero-hour contract. The reason for this is that after seven months of employment in the company, Paul and I feel that Stan has not produced the sales he should have. Realistically, the opportunities that the company has received so far are largely due to Paul and I running experiences at our events and explaining the tech to interested parties. Stan is essentially keeping James company during our trips and, when back home, it is difficult to trace whether Stan is actually working or not. This will save the company a further £1,800 a month.

The reduction in staff hours and directors' salaries is going to save a further £5,000 a month. The remaining actions are to make sure no important sums of money are being spent without all directors being in agreement.

I'm very much aware that sticking to this kind of spending every month when we have been spending over five times that amount is going to be incredibly difficult and require extreme hard work. The way I see it, though, is that we are nearly at the end of July and by the time we take the current liabilities out and the expected liabilities due for the next six month, such as Liverpool rent, we have about £120k of available funds for the next five months. We do not have any choice.

Aside from the Financial Rescue Plan, we discuss a data leakage with one of our potential customers that could be detrimental to the company. There are now at least two other companies similar to us who want a piece of this market. We also discuss an issue where James gave Stan a non-sealed envelope containing all the staff and directors' salary cheques to be counter-signed by either me or Paul which he could have easily taken a look at.

Next on the agenda is our new business account. A couple of month ago, we received confirmation that our new company bank account with NatWest was now open. I'm not sure exactly why we needed to change bank accounts, as we have had our current bank account with Barclays Bank since early 2015, but I have other things to worry about other than what bank we are using or why we need a different one.

However, to add insult to injury, during that meeting, Paul requests that he and I should have access to this new business account, as this has not been organised yet. James advises that this is not possible, as the shareholders of the company are concerned about the use of funds. James has made a verbal agreement to them to remain the sole steward of the business bank account until December.

What an incredible eye-popping statement, considering that James is actually the one spending most of the company's money! We manage to agree that we will be given a detailed bank statement every single month from now on.

It is also at this time that I decide to put a payroll system in place. James has been saying for months that he is going to organise payslips, but our staff have now been working for us for over six months without any payslip whatsoever. So, I take the decision to subscribe to a local payroll software company and started to produce all payslips for all staff including the backdated ones up to the beginning of the year.

Another important thing discussed at the board meeting is our UK company. James mentioned a few times in the past that it would be better to operate the Liverpool studio as a UK-based company (as the main company is based in Jersey, an offshore island with different regulations.) I am not at all aware of what the differences are between a UK mainland-based company and a Jersey-based company. Sure, I understand that there are some taxation benefits from a VAT point of view and of course some regulations that must be different. Aside from that, I have no idea as to why running the Liverpool studio would be better under a UK-based company than our existing – already complex – structure in Jersey. Anyway, that's another thing I left to James and our lawyers to sort out since we have way more than enough to deal with already.

During that meeting, James informs us that the UK company has been open for a few weeks now and gives us the registration details and registered address. He explains that the whole Liverpool studio lease, spending and revenues will now be processed under this company. It is at this moment that our company secretary, who must have done some research in advance, interrupts James and asks him why he is the sole director of the UK company and why Paul and I are not mentioned as shareholders. This is in breach of the original shareholder agreement!

Neither Paul nor I know that the UK company is already established, so we also don't know that we are not shareholders. Our well-prepared company secretary then hands over two forms to me and Paul and tells us to complete them, return them to her and she will arrange for us to be added as shareholders.

On that note, the meeting ends. Paul and I reconvene a little later to discuss what just happened. It's funny how a single day in a whole year can be such a turning point. Not only is this the start of our Financial Rescue Plan which would hopefully save the company, but, more importantly, this is definitely the day where we feel we can no longer trust James.

Paul and my trust in James has been fading away rapidly in recent months, but the behaviour shown with regards to the UK company handling is the nail in the coffin. From now on we both decide that we will be monitoring James very closely with the finances and will not trust anything he says.

Accordingly, during this meeting, we discuss the UK company shareholding and I tell Paul that I will personally not be signing the shareholding form just yet. He is free to go ahead if he wants, but considering that I do not know what being a shareholder in a UK company means, I need to investigate and understand the exact terms and implications.

Also, considering the fact that we have been left out of the Liverpool studio development and that the launch and near future of the studio look quite bleak, I decide that I do not want any more hassle for the time being than we already have. My decision is that before signing anything, I will be doing some more research. Paul agrees with me and he too does not sign or return the form. That is a good decision in hindsight: more on this later!

MY FAVORITE QUOTE

"Forecasts may tell you a great deal about the forecaster; they tell you nothing about the future."
Warren Buffett –American business magnate and investor.

LESSON LEARNED:

Well, I could not agree more with Warren Buffet. We all know that financial forecasts are very much a guess at the best of times.
In the case of an established company or one that follows existing trends or designs, it should be relatively straightforward to plan a financial forecast. In the case of a company like ours, however, involved in a brand-new industry which nobody knows where it is going yet (and, as time has proved, an industry that ended up being nowhere near as successful as so many experts initially had expected,) I don't see how it is possible to make any realistic forecasts.

So, in my view, our company forecast should have been more like a budget focusing on what we can spend and what we have. This is how I put our Financial Rescue Plan together.

WHAT WOULD YOU HAVE DONE?

1. Would you have signed the UK company shareholding agreement immediately and taken control of the events in Liverpool?

2. Would you have withheld signing, as we did, until being more aware of the regulations and differences between a UK and a Jersey company?

Or maybe you think completely differently? If so, please share what you would have done online at 1b1m1y.com

You can also log in to that website to view what other people would have done

CHAPTER NINETEEN

Blackmail?

A few days have passed since our last board meeting, and Paul and I have been busy implementing our Rescue Plan. It requires new updated staff contracts, new directors' forms for purchase orders as well as the creation of a new spreadsheet specifically to keep our new low budget as much as possible within our Rescue Plan.

On the 28th of July, we reconvene for our third board meeting that week. Strangely, as the meeting started and without any prior notice, James informs us he has been working on a new budget and he presents us with a "liabilities and spending forecast" which is a short-term view of how the company money needs to be spent in the coming months. He has essentially used the key elements of our Financial Rescue Plan to produce his own version!

Aside from a few changes in company spending, the main difference is that James categorically refuses to change Stan's contract to a zero-hour one.

Paul and my argument is that Stan has been with us for over seven months with pretty much no results to show for it, that he was overpaid "by mistake" at the beginning of the year by about £1,500 (which is yet to be paid back) and that he has also recently presented us with some phone bills in excess of £700 for "sales phone calls made abroad." I later find out that they are mainly personal phone calls! We then add the "party" performances on the various exhibitions and the fact that there is no sales plan for the Liverpool studio and end up with a question to James,
"How can Stan be considered a suitable salesperson for our company?"
He may have been the best car salesman in the past, but we feel that technology is not his strength. There is nothing personal in that decision; we all have our strengths and weaknesses and we can't be good at everything.

It is important also to highlight that we are not dismissing Stan, and, more importantly still, that our zero-hour contract proposal comes with an increased commission percentage. If Stan is able to sell, he will easily make up the shortfall of his fixed monthly salary. That does, however, require Stan to sell stuff.

Paul and I are a little dismayed about having one director working to produce his own rescue plan while he knows we are working to implement the one we proposed at our last meeting. Paul and I take a look at James' suggestions but, while it is much improved on the original forecast, we feel that it is still not realistic enough for the immediate survival of the business. After further discussion on how we can adjust our Rescue Plan to make it more flexible, we decide to carry the discussion over to the next meeting, scheduled for the following day, the 29th of July.

It's the fourth board meeting of the week! Before resuming our discussion about the Financial Rescue Plan, I raise a point that Brian from BroadMesse is looking to reduce the amount of equipment we would supply in any of their customer quotes. In fact, it has come to the point where Brian is looking for us to provide our wireless VR headset only alongside transmitters. This will have a drastic reduction in potential income for the business, as we are not making a huge amount of profit on the headset alone.

Each headset is made of a main circuit board that feeds the high-resolution screen and is connected to our wireless receiver board. (See photos page 162.)

It is then manually built into a 3D printed headset that has been finished in a carbon look. This is then supplied with a video transmitter, two high capacity batteries, all cables and a case – costing us around £2,000 to produce. So, even if we did sell them for twice that amount – which would actually be expensive from our Chinese customer point of view – it would not be very worthwhile.

As the situation regarding the agreement between the company and BroadMesse is unclear, it is resolved that James will contact Mr Dong for a resolution.

Next on the agenda is a concern from James of not having heard from the universities for a little while. Paul replies that a conference call is organised with both universities as per recent emails, to James' surprise.

It transpires that James has not received any emails for days as, at some point, he has been cut from the communication loop.

As Paul is the main person behind the negotiations between the two universities, it seems that one of our correspondents at the University of Nebraska started to email Paul only and forgot to copy James in. This was not picked up until now. James gets cross with the situation and tells Paul that he should have consulted me and James before agreeing to a meeting time and date. He says it is out of order to proceed this way.

As I have never met with the Nebraska team, I am not really involved with the university negotiations, so I let Paul talk himself out of this one. The reason I mention this anecdote is because, with hindsight, it is quite funny how James got upset about a decision being made without his knowledge, yet he had been doing that so many times with us in the past. Nothing like a bit of your own medicine to understand the problem sometimes . . .

It's now the beginning of August 2016. Paul and I have worked flat out over the last few days to finalise and implement the Financial Rescue Plan which includes writing new staff contracts.

We then organise a meeting with our entire team to introduce our Financial Rescue Plan that included a reduction in their hours – and their pay – accordingly.

Needless to say, this is received with some anger from some of the staff. I go on to explain the situation the company is in, I explain the details of the planned budget for the coming months and I make a point to clearly explain that, although we have to take drastic action, we also have some amazing opportunities lined up so this will just be a rough patch and we will be back to normal hours and salary as soon as possible.

Something odd happens during that two-hour meeting. As I am explaining the situation and the different points of the Rescue Plan to the staff, Paul – who is sitting next to me – is adding some details here and there. Meanwhile, James has chosen to sit between two of our staff members opposite me and Paul and, during the meeting, James makes a few remarks picking on our Rescue Plan as well as a few inappropriate comments with regards to where the company is, financially.

This greatly annoys me, as James is clearly trying to make himself look like the "good guy" with the staff while Paul and I are the "evil directors" who have spent all of the company's money and are now having to make drastic savings, including staff salaries.

I am quite close during that meeting to asking James to leave the room, but it would have been very unprofessional to have an argument with James in front of all the staff. We let him have his ego boosting moment and end the meeting shaking everyone's hands and thanking them for their support.

The week is completed with a fifth and final board meeting shortly after our staff meeting where James clearly exposes his views to us.

Thankfully, Paul, as usual, is recording the meeting and that is a good thing.

That meeting does not last long, but Paul and I are told, in very explicit terms by James, that he is not in agreement with our Rescue Plan and, more importantly, does not agree to change Stan's contract to a zero-hour one. With hindsight, we can only assume that, for personal reasons, James could not be seen as "letting his friend down" and was going to fight for him.

The short meeting is quite heated and James has a good go at me and Paul in a fairly aggressive tone and attitude trying to make us change our minds on a few points on our Rescue Plan. When he realises that Paul and I are going to stick to our guns, he shouts out,

"OK guys! So this is how you want to play it? Well, if you don't remove the zero-hour contract condition, then I will not raise any more money for this company!" He storms out of the office, nearly breaking the door as he smashes it so hard!

"Did you record that?" I say to Paul.

"Oh yes, it's in the can," he confirms. We have reached a new level in our company. Are Paul and I now being blackmailed by James to go along with what he wants?

It is incredible for three directors to get to that stage but, in some ways, it is not surprising. James has been so used to getting what he wants since the beginning without even consulting Paul or me for the majority of decisions. Now that we are finally putting a control on him, he feels he is losing control, and I believe this is what triggered that reaction.

We never talk about that meeting again, but eventually all of the Financial Rescue Plan actions are implemented, including company purchase order forms for any spending above £50 requiring two directors' signature and any spending above £500 requiring three directors' signature. Well, everything except the zero-hour contract for Stan. Yes, James did get his way once again!

However, it wasn't just an acceptance from Paul and me to remove that condition. This decision came after a serious bargaining offer from James. I'll tell you more in the next chapter

MY FAVORITE QUOTE

"Risk comes from not knowing what you are doing."
Warren Buffett –American business magnate and investor.

LESSON LEARNED:

I've selected another quote from Warren Buffet, as he once said, "Never invest in a business you cannot understand."

We knew from the onset that James was not technologically-minded and knew very little about the tech involved in virtual reality, but my view was that we all have a job to do and we can't be good at everything so I was fine with that. Considering James not only had a wealth of experience in the finance industry, but also had the trust of some wealthy investors prepared to put a large sum of money in our business, this was good enough for me.

However, as per the previous few chapters, Paul and I had already started to smell a rat early on at the end of February. By the end of April, the additional events meant we definitely knew something was not right and yet it took us until nearly the end of July to finally blow out and put a stop to it.

What we should have done is raise our concerns much earlier on and called an EGM (Extraordinary General Meeting) with the shareholders and investors to put our concerns on the table.

The only reason we did not do this is because we felt that James had the trust of the investors and we felt he knew what he was doing. Even if we did not agree with his way of doing things, we did not want to overstep our position and create a possible breakdown of trust and relationship. Of course, with hindsight, it is easy to see that we should have called that EGM!

WHAT WOULD YOU HAVE DONE?

1. In the title of this chapter, I am suggesting that this could be seen as blackmail. It is a strong word and I am not saying it was, but how do you see that? Would you qualify this attitude as blackmailing the directors?

2. Or do you think that it was just a serious director clash and, combined with the mounting company problems, was just tempers going a little wild?

Or maybe you think completely differently? If so, please share what you would have done online at 1b1m1y.com

You can also log in to that website to view what other people would have done

CHAPTER TWENTY

Opportunities . . . more opportunities

The first couple of weeks of August have gone by quite rapidly and since it is always a quiet month for business in general, many of us have taken the opportunity to go on annual leave.

During my holiday in the south of France, I take the opportunity to go back to see our contacts at the CNES to finalise the agreement.

On my return, now that the Financial Rescue Plan is in motion, I am keen to focus on finalising the many opportunities we have on the boil. Since more opportunities are about to open up, I am really keen to put the recent difficult events behind us, learn from them and start on a fresh path to get this company the success it deserves.

It's the 15th of August 2016. We start this month's board meeting by raising the point that none of our staff members have returned their signed amended contract with the reduction of hours. We agree to wait another week before chasing this up.

The first good news of August comes with James announcing MerciaTech's interest in investing in our company. It is early days, but James is in touch with them and looking to organise a meeting next month. As a side note, MerciaTech is a very large venture capital firm that invests in tech businesses and they have recently invested £5.1million in a VR content development firm called nDreams. Having researched the company, we could be a match made in heaven. We have a very new offering, nDreams are VR content developers and MerciaTech are looking to invest in growing companies. This could not have come at a better time.

This is very welcome news as I have been feeling a little down with the recent weeks' events. While I am not one to give up in life, I have been considering many possible scenarios for our company's next few months and they don't look great. The possibility of the company closing before the end of the year is very real.

James also introduces us to a lady – a marketing professional – who is willing to take on the marketing of our Liverpool studio.

As per the Financial Rescue Plan, we have now started to refurbish our studio a little to make it more welcoming to visitors in preparation for opening it on weekends.

Aside from being "raw" looking, our studio is brilliant. We have a huge open space of nearly 200 square metres (2,100 square feet) fully kitted out with our tracking system and F1 racing simulator, as well as a corner where our working desks are.

It's not customer-friendly so we get the caretaker of the premises to build a low-cost partition to separate it into sections, install a couple of sofas and make it a spectator area so we can start to open our experiences to the public. Of course, this is our workshop where we are developing our products, but the technology is good enough to be paid for. James is not keen on this, but Paul and I feel like it is a low-cost transformation that will easily be paid back with the first income.

Also, as far as opportunities are concerned, we are certainly not short of them. We have recently received a visit from the managing director of Attraktion, an Austria-based manufacturer of 4D and 5D theme park attractions. They like what we do and would like to expand their offering with a VR branch. After a long meeting, they feel we could have a good partnership, but more on this later!

We have also been invited to Bahrain to attend a one-week event to launch a new shopping mall. This is all expenses paid as well as full rental charge for our equipment. It looks great and will be another reference to what we do, as well as bringing in around £12,000 profit for that week.

We are also considering whether we should attend the Dubai GITEX in October. A few months ago, when we were out to attend as many exhibitions as possible, we thought attending it would be a good idea, as well as another show close by called the Rich Boys' Toys exhibition.

We have paid a deposit for it, but considering we're not only due to pay the balance on the exhibition costs but also need to pay for the flights, hotel and shipping our equipment there, this is going to be a big burden when we are trying to keep our monthly spending below £17k. It would be a shame to miss out on it, but it just does not look like we are going to be able to afford it.

The Rich Boys' Toys exhibition would have been especially good for us, as our F1 simulator is now working very nicely. We've had a number of people testing it, even some professional racing drivers, and the feedback has been very good. I haven't talked about our F1 simulator much so far, but this was my baby from the start and one of the two ideas discussed during the first few meetings between Paul and me early in 2014.

As a fan of Formula 1 and as a fan of simulation games, I thought having a F1 experience where you sit in a whole F1 car replica, put on a real racing helmet that has been converted to be a high-resolution VR headset and race around a track with a powerful motion platform moving around to give you g-force feedback would be an amazing feeling.

I'm not talking about the kind of motion platforms that vibrate or move sharply around when you turn. No! What I wanted to achieve was something smooth and powerful so when you accelerate the platform tilts up 25 degrees, you fall back in your seat and feel your own weight pushing on your back. Equally, when braking, the platform would tilt forward, sending your body sharply forward, only restrained by the seat harness. When taking fast corners, the platform would roll sideways to the opposite direction of the turns, pushing your whole body against the car sides. If this sounds weird, it's simply because it is! You see, using the techniques described above have the effect of tricking the brain into thinking you are in that fast car. As the eyes only see what the VR headset shows them, the tricks used above, with the help of the powerful motion platform, mean the brain associates the forces felt as being real g-force (which they are not, of course.) It all contributes to an amazing experience.

The above, combined with a full staged F1 garage, a two-way pit-to-driver communication device and the ability to race your friends would be offered as a truly unique and realistic F1 experience.

As a side note, while this was my concept from the start, having been away so much and having so many balls to juggle, I have tried to remain involved with the progress and development on a regular basis, but credit where it's due. The simulator would not be as close to what I wanted it to be by now if it weren't for the amazing work of our developer Frank assisted by Mikey.

The only thing we need now is our final VR helmet headset. We have had a prototype for a while and our final VR helmet is now in design. By the time it is completed, we will have a completely unique ready-to-sell product!

We also discuss our amazing opportunity to create a unique custom tracking system based on CNES' technology. The agreement is based on a licence, so we will have to pay the CNES around £50,000 a year in royalties as a minimum, increasing if the sales are higher than the agreed minimum. We have worked out that this will be easily made up, considering the large cost of the tracking system we are currently using versus this new technology.

Our profit on the current Vicon Optical tracking system is quite low, with about 20% profit margin on the hardware. Using this new technology means we could retail a full tracking system at about a quarter of the price and still make the same profit margin.

Three weeks later, it is the 7th of September. Business life has now resumed after the summer holidays, so things are starting to move a bit quicker.

Our first board meeting of September is busy as usual. Firstly, James confirms that a meeting between him and Mike Hayes at MerciaTech has been secured for the 20th of this month.

James asks me to prepare a secure online vault where we can put all of our investment documents to be shared with MerciaTech.

As mentioned previously, our Financial Rescue Plan is now in full swing, except for Stan's zero-hour contract. What happened is that James was so adamant that he was not going to allow his mate to be side-tracked that he ended up

1 Business, 1 Million, 1 Year

offering a cut on his own salary by 50%. We agreed to put this towards Stan's salary.

Also, the MD of Attraktion, who I mentioned earlier, has been in touch regularly with us since his visit three weeks ago. He would like us to be present on their booth at the IAAPA (International Association of Amusement Park and Attractions) exhibition in Barcelona which takes place in two weeks on the 20th, 21st and 22nd of September.

This is very short notice and we are going to need to organise a quick turnaround to be able to attend. Considering he is offering to pay up to £5,000 towards the cost of the trip, and that firms up our agreement with Attraktion to become one of their suppliers, this is too good an opportunity to miss.

It is decided that Stan and Frank – our developer – will join me and James in Barcelona. Paul and I argue with James as to why there needs to be four of us on site, but it all falls on deaf ears as usual with some excuses as to why our salesman is required to be there!

Finally, as we are reaching the AOB (Any Other Business) part of the agenda, we are informed by James that two of our investor shareholders have decided to become non-executive board members and directors due to concerns about the company's finances. I am delighted with the idea, as I think it will be very good for the investors to see what is happening from our side. Paul and I are not convinced they are being presented with accurate information.

MY FAVORITE QUOTE

"If you are not embarrassed by the first version of your product, you've launched too late."
Reid Hoffman – co-founder of LinkedIn.

LESSON LEARNED:

I've chosen that quote here in relation to our F1 simulator. You see, we've had a couple of meetings recently with the whole team, as Stan seems to struggle to sell the F1 experience concept.

The whole simulator is now nearly ready. There is a little more work to be done on the commercial version of our VR helmet as well as some finishing adjustments on the overall presentation of the product, but I feel it is nearly there. I would comfortably say that we are around three months away from having a commercially ready-to-sell product which, in the meantime, can be tested and evaluated.

Yet Stan seems to be coming up with excuse after excuse that he cannot sell it as it does not feel ready to be sold. However, I'm sure with a little effort we could secure some pre-orders that would be crucial to the company's finances.

WHAT WOULD YOU HAVE DONE?

1. Would you agree with me that the time was right to start pushing the simulator sales – even three months away from it being commercially ready – as we are able to offer a very good experience to anyone wanting to try it? This could help us secure some pre-orders, maybe even at a special early orders price.

2. Would you say that it is better to wait until the product is fully commercially ready and all finished to start selling it?

Or maybe you think completely differently? If so, please share what you would have done online at 1b1m1y.com

You can also log in to that website to view what other people would have done

CHAPTER TWENTY ONE

The importance of due diligence

Ten days later, aside from another board meeting on the 13th for more talk about opportunities and actions plans, we have been flat out organising our last-minute trip to Barcelona. Since it was too late to book a shipping company to get our kit there on time, we hire a local driver and van to take it all the way to Barcelona and back for us while we are flying there.

During the meeting on the 13th, James hands me a USB stick with all our company's portfolio documents and due diligence paperwork for me to copy into the secure vault. This is so that an online link and login credentials can be provided to MerciaTech to review following the meeting with James in a few days. On this USB, aside from the pitch deck that Paul and I put together after the Oppenheimer meeting and our company brochures that I prepared for our two products which are, essentially sale sheets explaining what the Motion Studio VR F1 simulator is, there is also our company's business plan and forecast that James put together in the past. There is also the directors' personal information and all the company's other legal agreements, such as structure, shareholding, and, of course, our patent-pending applications, trademarks and copyrights which are the backbone of the company from an investment point of view.

We also discuss a quote we received from the marketing lady in Liverpool asking for £3,500 per month for the next four months that will cover one week's work per month. James is keen to go ahead with this as our Liverpool studio launch happened two months ago pretty much to the day and no interest and no sales have taken place. While Paul and I can see the need to market the studio, we still feel that it is not targeted at the right audience and, as such, spending that kind of money per month is ludicrous. We also don't feel that this lady is the right person. We've had a couple of meetings with her and she has not given us the feeling that she fully understands what we are trying to achieve or what the whole product is about, but we might be wrong!

Also during that meeting, Paul points out that an error had been made in the reduction of staff hours, costing us an extra £451 a month. James states with a smile that this is not going to be an amount that would take the company into liquidation and that he is confident he will be able to raise additional money for the company.

To end the meeting on a positive note, we have now received the signed sales agreement from our first client, Igor in Indonesia. This is the first part of a large installation, initially for a 2 vs 2 players across an 8 metre x 5 metre area. The total contract is worth £56,000, a 50% deposit will be paid shortly by the client and we are due to organise the installation on site in early November.

The company is looking to be over the worst. We have now secured our first customer sale, we have a number of opportunities in hand and there is a very exciting investment prospect in process.

Two days later, we've arrived late afternoon in Barcelona for the IAAPA exhibition. To keep costs low and make sure we fit everything in the allocated budget, we've rented an Airbnb four-bedroom property to share.

First thing the following morning, we head straight to the Gran Via Convention Centre to set up our booth. We are under the branding of our sponsor and partner Attraktion. By mid-afternoon, our 7 metre x 5 metre booth is set up and we're ready to go for the next three days.

It is yet another very busy event. The IAAPA is known internationally and held three times a year in various countries around the world. It is *the* exhibition to attend for any attraction or amusement industry owner or operator.

Overall, it is a successful event with great feedback. The way we operate our experiences is that one of us always walks around the tracked area to supervise the VR users. It is important, as the users cannot see the outside world and only go with what they see on the headset. Of course, our content is designed and adapted to fit the area we have to make sure the user does not walk into real walls, but there are the occasional users who want to see if they can walk through virtual walls (which they can) or try things that they should not do. When they do this, it takes them close to the tracking boundary and possibly dangerous areas such as walls or management consoles.

At this stage, we are working on the now very common "guardian" feature that shows the VR limit in the headset. This was not ready at the

time and I recall one hiccup very clearly. While
Stan is supervising a customer walking around
our VR content, he takes his eyes of the ball and
the customer ends up going into a real wall and
hurting his nose which is bleeding slightly.
Thankfully, the customer takes it lightly and
laughs about it, but it goes to show how
important the supervision of the experiences is
and it seems that Stan could not even be trusted
to do that!

James has to fly back early to attend the
MerciaTech meeting so on the last day we pack
everything up, wave goodbye to our van driver
who will be taking our equipment back home
and I take my two colleagues Francois and Stan
for dinner. Barcelona is a very lively city, so we
jump in a taxi and head down to the marina and
settle on one of the many restaurants on the
harbour. I've got an expense sheet that I am
keeping to make sure we stay within the
allocated budget and the shipping, flat rental,
flights and transfer have already used 90% of it,
while the last few nights' dinners and drinks
have pretty much used the remainder. I settle
the cost of that dinner on the company card and
this brings our total expenses to pretty much
within the £5,000 budget given by Attraktion.
After the meal, we walk back along the harbour
and stop at one of the many bars. Stan asks for a
round which I agree to pay for as it just fits
within the remaining budget – it's also a thank

you for their work over the last three days. However, after the first round, I get prompted several times to get us a few more on the company card, which I categorically refuse since it would go over our budget which is neither approved, nor wise spending.

If we did not have a suitable company name already, I would possibly rename us "Opportunity VR." The reason for this is that, aside from the many opportunities we've already had during the year so far, we are about to receive another 15 new enquiries following the Barcelona event. There is a chain of casinos that is keen to hear more about the simulator; a large aquarium in Dubai that is an existing client of Attraktion who is keen for us to develop a custom underwater VR experience; we have an initial contact with the team setting up the Ferrari experience in Tarragona, Spain, which is due to open early in 2017; and many other enquiries from small and medium entertainment locations around France, Spain, Corsica, Italy and even as far as Hungary. Estimates are flying out of the window and we have many sales opportunities building up now which is great for the company and for morale considering the events of the last few months.

The small downfall with receiving these dozens of new enquiries is that Stan has never bothered taking the time to learn or understand our technology or, more importantly, our costs and margins. This means every single quotation request that we receive has to be designed and customised by me or Paul, taking time away from other things we need to do. Stan should have – by now after nine months with us – be the one managing and following these enquiries.

On our return from Barcelona, we have a quick meeting between Paul, James and me to catch up. We discuss the event in Barcelona and see how the important investment meeting between James and MerciaTech went. It will come as no surprise to you by now that this ended up being yet another missed opportunity. We did not know that yet, but it would become quickly obvious that there was no feedback or communication from Mike Hayes or MerciaTech after that initial meeting. Obviously, following the previous fiasco with Oppenheimer a few month before, Paul and I are very concerned as to what James asked at the meeting or how he actually "sold" it. The reason is much more simple. A few weeks later, Paul is speaking to a gentleman that he knows who is not only very well connected in the tech world, but is also an private investor in various tech as well as an executive officer in one of the major Silicon Valley companies. As we casually discuss our investment offer in a hope that he may be interested in investing personally, he decides to take a look at our portfolio and due diligence documents.

His feedback is quite shocking! Firstly, our pitch deck is too long and not clear enough, our business plan is not a business plan but a kind of company resumé, our forecast is worthless as it does not take into consideration the many ramifications of our planned expansion and as for our due diligence, it is missing a lot of information on the directors, and overall company documents, agreements, structure and so on. His words are, "Our portfolio does not show our company in a very professional way!"

Paul and I are stunned! We're not even sure what to say to each other. We thought James had put all those documents in place – since he had been due to do that for many months now – and surely the large amount of money we spent on our lawyer would have produced all the legal documents?

OK, sure. You are going to say that, by now, Paul and I had had our fair share of warning that James was not to be trusted and we should have taken a closer look at the portfolio and due diligence documents. You would be right, we should have done that, but, in our defence, we have been flat out preparing the order for our first client in Indonesia. Paul and I are due on site in Jakarta in the first week of November and the full order has to be shipped by the 10th of October at the latest in order to give it enough time to get there, but, more importantly to clear any custom duty and possible issues. We've had barely three weeks since confirmation of the order and our return from Barcelona to get four brand-new headsets built. Just for clarification, we now have all the electronic parts as well as the 3D printed parts in house and we build the headset ourselves. It takes us about three hours on each headset at this stage. We also have to order a full tracking system from Vicon. On the day of the order, we are told by our Vicon contact that they are closing for two weeks for stocktaking, so if we need an order it has to be placed today or we will have to wait two weeks. Well, no time to mess around. I check with Paul, who is next to me, and we confirm the order – an order I will end up being blamed for later on!

That order also requires us to prepare our props which are large toy rifles that we dismantle and get every plastic part customised in a carbon look by using the hydro dipping technique. This applies a durable film all over which gives our rifle a stunning shiny carbon finish. We then build the tracking LEDs and the wireless trigger inside the rifle before putting it all back together. Finally, we have to prepare and customise the software to integrate with our client's own content, all of the cabling, manuals and many other parts and, as this is our first proper customer order, we have spread it all out on our studio floor to make sure we have an inventory of every bit we need and to make sure we do not forget anything.

So, yes, between handling the short-term notice preparation for Barcelona, attending the exhibition, preparing the numerous estimates following the event, building the new headsets and props, keeping up with the current developments on the simulators and VR helmet and preparing our first order, the last two weeks have been insanely busy. We have not had the time to prepare documents or check that everything is in order with them and, even if we did have the time, I'm not entirely sure I would know what is needed.

Anyway, right or wrong, the fact is that our investment portfolio is not up to scratch. This means the likely reason we never heard back from MerciaTech is because they though exactly the same as our Silicon Valley executive contact. Or maybe James put them off by asking for another ridiculous amount of money. Or maybe both – who knows! The point is that we have lost another investment chance and another chance to turn over the company's fortunes! Is James actually on a mission to sabotage our company by any means possible?

It is the 29th of September. At this board meeting we are joined by two of our shareholders who will be appointed as directors in the company during the meeting. I am so happy this is happening, and I feel that if this had occurred many months ago, things may have likely been different.

Aside from now being a five-director board, we also review many more opportunities that are due to be finalised. We have a customer from New Zealand who is keen to use our technology to sell their kitchen developments, the French guys are also getting ready to open their large arcade and we would be fitting in over £200k worth of VR equipment there. We've also recently returned from a trip to our Liverpool studio where James and I had a meeting with the executive team of Enterspace who are based in Sweden. They really like our products and feel it could offer the technology they need to launch their multiusers 'pod' style systems which offers space-based VR experiences for museums and entertainment centres. Each location will require 40-50 headsets per site and they are expecting to receive funding in Q1 of 2017.

There is also Prakash from ASI World in Dubai who we met in Shanghai a few months back. He offers custom entertainment attractions to many locations throughout the world and we have been discussing an option for him to become a distributor of our products.

Finally, we also look at our finances – or what's left of them! There is just over £100k left in our bank account with the latest liabilities paid. We're due to receive around £7,500 back from our local government in local import taxes that we paid for purchases. James completed the application form a few months ago and, once we're GST registered, we will be able to receive that money back. That will turn out to be another fiasco. I'm not entirely sure why, but James is having a couple of meetings in the coming weeks with a lady from the tax office and we end up being informed that our company does not qualify for GST registration at this stage.

There is also confirmation that the sale of our F1 motion platform that is stored in the UK is finalised for an amount of £12k. Unfortunately, this is not even a third of what we paid for it six months ago, but, as the saying goes, "Beggars can't be choosers." At this stage, £12k income is better than nothing!

Finally, we're just about to receive our first client's deposit of £26k, which will be followed by another £26k once installation is complete. If we are careful, we will be fine.

MY FAVORITE QUOTE

"Diligence is the mother of good luck."
**Benjamin Franklin – a Founding Father of the
United States.**

LESSON LEARNED:

This quote may be interpreted differently by
people, but, for me, it goes with my belief that
success has more to do with careful planning,
hard work and consistence than just pure luck.

I do agree that many life opportunities can
happen thanks to being in the right place at the
right time ; however, it is what you do with these
opportunities that defines their success or
failure. In our case, we have created some strong
investment opportunities and yet we are
jeopardising them one after another because we
do not have a due diligence in place.

WHAT WOULD YOU HAVE DONE?

1. Would you agree that our due diligence pack and investment portfolio was not up to scratch when it should have been and it is obvious that we did not get any response from the investment opportunity?

2. Or do you think that due diligence pack and investment portfolio are not the "be all and end all" and there are more to it than that and the company products, structure and future plans are more important?

Or maybe you think completely differently? If so, please share what you would have done online at 1b1m1y.com

You can also log in to that website to view what other people would have done

CHAPTER TWENTY TWO

Our first sale

Two weeks have passed. It is the 13th of October, we are having another one of our board meetings, but this time only four directors are present as James is away.

During the meeting, we discuss our trip to Jakarta and the installation due in just over two weeks. Paul and I will be flying Emirates to Dubai and then on to Jakarta. While I am cautious at this stage about booking expensive business class flights, we actually manage to get two return flights in business class all the way to Jakarta (18 hours) for £2,200 each. Considering that the client is invoiced for the cost of installation and travel and considering that we are on site for only five days and we will need to be actively operational, flying business class is the wise option.

Our two new directors are very active at getting up to speed with the day-to-day operation of the business. They want to know the profit margin we are working on when quoting customers and they suggest some ideas in purchasing our hardware in different currencies. This may save us some conversion costs especially on the large items that cost several thousands of pounds.

We also review the status of our products. The VR studio is now ready to be sold and we have actually made our first sale, the F1 simulator is now about two months away from being a fully finished product and they agree that it is in a position where we should be able to take pre-orders. There is a concern that we have a remaining £10k to pay to our VR helmet designers, but, once done, the VR simulator will be a product ready to sell.

We are planning to retail it at £120k allowing a margin for discounts. The completed simulator with the motion platform, full F1 replica chassis in custom client paint work, two high-resolution VR helmets, the control station, the content and the extras such as the spectator viewing screens, the props, the two-way radio system, installation and training is costing us around £85k. This gives

us around a 30% profit margin without any
discount applied.

Considering that in an ideal world, an
entertainment centre would be offering at least
two, but often three or four simulators at the
same time so customers can race together on
the same track, this means that we could make
between £60k and £100k of profit per sale.
Added to that, we have the yearly licence we will
be charging for support, and content updates are
expected to be around £1,500 per simulator.

It may seem a little expensive, but a standard
gaming arcade machine, such as the Mario Kart
driving simulator which is operated with £1
coins, costs around £12k to purchase. Our
simulator is offering a unique experience lasting
25 minutes with, on average, ten minutes in the
driving seat (the rest of the time is spent fitting
the racing suit and helmet,) the briefing, the
installation in the cockpit and then the
debriefing afterwards with full telemetry and
expert advice on how to improve your lap times.
Of course, clients will be free to charge whatever
they want, but we are suggesting a
recommended retail price of £20 for the 25-
minute experience in line with real go-kart
pricings.

We have also prepared a return on investment
plan which shows that, based on an average of

four users per hour – as while someone is in the driving seat, the next client is being briefed and the previous client is being debriefed – and with an average occupancy of 50% (or in other words, the simulator being used fully on five hours out of ten hours per day, seven days a week,) the client will get his ROI (Return On Investment) after one year operating the simulator. If we add to that the extras that can be sold alongside the experience such as on-board photos and videos (that combine the user's racing experience with cleverly positioned external cameras making it look like he really is at the wheel of a racing car) as well as the various merchandise that can be offered such as caps, t-shirts and various F1 memorabilia, each simulator can generate in excess of £120k gross profits per year.

There is simply nothing out there anywhere near as advanced and as realistic at this time. As a side note, nearly two and half years on, I am yet to try something that comes close to the experience we built back then.

Yes, there are lots of VR simulators available nowadays, but most of them use just a single open seat attached to some good – or not so good – motion platforms with an off-the-shelf VR headset. For some reason, the majority seem to insist on providing vibrations and sharp movements which I find annoying and unpleasant while driving.

I've never had the privilege to sit in a real Formula 1 car, but one of the professional racing drivers who tests our platform explains to us that real racing cars like an F1 do not overly vibrate and do not throw you right and left. They are smooth and clean and the only thing you really feel is the g-force as you accelerate, brake or go flat out around a corner. This is what we have aimed to build.

As you sit in our F1 simulator and the engine starts, you can feel it purring in your back as well as in your hands when holding the steering wheel with micro vibrations that we've added on the up and down axis. As you accelerate, that vibration increases, but it is kept gentle.

However, what we use the motion platform excellent acceleration and velocity performances for is to trick your brain into thinking you are driving fast, breaking hard and taking corners at a very high speed. The effect is so efficient that after driving around the track for 15 minutes, you feel the pain in your neck and arms as if you had suffered from repeated g-forces

However, we also understand that it can be a fairly big investment to some companies so we have also been developing a similar version based on the same content and same motion algorithm, but this one only has a racing seat on it (no F1 chassis) and does have a little less angular velocity and acceleration. The experience is still great, however, and works with our existing content, control panel and VR helmet. That platform cost us £19k to produce, so we are planning to retail it in the region of £28k so this will be the affordable and lower space requirement version of our big F1 simulator.

Back to our four-director meeting! As we show our two new directors the latest version of our wireless headset, as well as the design and 3D models of our VR helmet in production, one of them asks whether the design, technology and concept of the headsets is protected. Paul and I respond that, yes, we spoke to a patent and trademark lawyer many months back together with James and, as far as we are aware, it is all in hand.

They also ask whether our logo and company name are trademarked which Paul and I are unable to confirm. They ask us to check and report back.

Next on the agenda is a concern that our next three months' rent payment is due for the Liverpool studio in five days. It amounts to just over £10k and the new directors ask us to show them a revenue sheet for the Liverpool studio so far to see how much of that rent we have been able to offset with revenue. We are unable to produce this, since no revenue has been received since the Liverpool studio opened three months ago.

The two directors ask how long the Liverpool studio lease is for and if it can be terminated early. Paul confirms that it is a three-year lease and, as far as we are aware, there are no early breaks possible. They keep firing questions at us with regards to Liverpool such as,
"How much marketing has been done for the studio?", "What is the value of the assets in the Liverpool studio?", "Is there a business plan in place?", "Is there a strategy?"
One of them says that he has been told by James that Stan is actively involved with the Liverpool studio's marketing to obtain leads, so what is the status on that?

At that stage, I interrupt the now quite annoyed directors to say that we should carry this question over for when James is able to attend the next committee meeting. He will hopefully be able to provide them with a fuller answer than we can since he has been overseeing the Liverpool studio from the start!

The decision is also made that we will not be attending the GITEX and the Rich Boys' Toys events in Dubai. It is a shame, as we have paid around £30k in total so far for those events. However, our funds are so limited that shipping the equipment, travelling there and attending the event would use a big chunk of the remainder of our finances right now. It is with deep regrets – especially as our nearly finished F1 simulator would have been the star of the Rich Boys' Toys show – that the decision is made not to attend.

If you recall in the previous chapter, I mentioned that the decision for me and Paul to place the order for the tracking system for our Jakarta client was going to be argued. Well, it happens at this meeting. You see, the two new directors have been busy in the last two weeks reviewing the company finances and the overall running of the company, hence the above questions as well as the next one. They ask Paul and me why over £20k has been spent purchasing hardware for the Jakarta client without the three directors' signatures as per the Financial Rescue Plan we submitted and implemented in August.

We apologise, but on that occasion, it was an executive decision that we had to make in order to make sure we would be able to receive the equipment on time. We had only hours spare to place the order and James was not contactable at the time. So, yes, it was wrong, but if we had not been able to get the tracking equipment on time, we would not have been able to ship on time. This would have most likely delayed the

Jakarta installation, so it wasn't an ideal situation.

We close that meeting and agree to have the next one in a week's time as we need to keep a very close eye on what is happening.

Just a week later, we have another board meeting. It is the 20th of October and we are joined by one of our investors on the phone as he is currently in the US.

It is a brief meeting and, essentially, the shareholders warn that as investors, they are not prepared to add any more funds to the company finances as originally suggested. Up until now, we knew we were in a critical situation financially, but, since James confidently told us that he was going to raise additional funds and since we knew there was a £600k potential loan note package as per the initial investment offer, we were hopeful that now we had a Financial Rescue Plan in place things were looking up for the company. Our first sale is confirmed and our second product is nearly ready for sale. We have a good number of serious opportunities and the investors are willing to release at least half of that amount so as to make sure the company capitalises on its work and opportunities.

This announcement is obviously a cold shower for us. Don't get me wrong, I have known since I put the Financial Rescue Plan in place two and half months ago that things were critical and that the company was on dangerous grounds. I even told our staff that if things did not change drastically, we would all be out of work by December. However, since I am someone who never ever gives up and as we have worked harder than ever before and as we have managed to keep nearly in line with the budget and are only over by about £8,000, I was hoping that if the investors could put in another £150k or so, this would buy us time on this budget until March or April 2017. By then, I was confident that the company's fortunes would be very different.

But it is quite clear that by joining us on the board three weeks ago, the investors / directors did their homework and realised that the company's finances had been seriously mismanaged. It worries them that adding more funds will only end up the same way as the million pounds they have already invested.

So, now that we know where we all are, and we know that we have very little room to manoeuvre, we just have to hope that we can secure another sale in the short-term and keep spending as little as possible.

It's the end of October. Paul and I have packed our bags and we're heading for a 24-hour trip to

Jakarta. This includes an hour's flight to London, a couple of hours' wait for our connection and a few more hours' wait in Dubai for our second connection.

This is the first time I am flying on the Airbus A380. This is an amazing jet. Having just flown business class for the first time earlier that year with all our flights so far on British Airways, I have been amazed by the business class service provided. However, I did not think it could be even better! The experience, of course, starts in the exclusive Emirates lounge at Gatwick Airport, then the business class seat on board of the A380 is fabulous. There's a very large screen, a fully flat bed, a personal counter with iPad-like tablets and your very own mini drinks shelf.

One of the anecdotes that still makes me smile to this day happens after take-off. I guess they must say this to all their passengers, but the hostess comes to my seat to hand over the menu for the evening and asks me whether I will be having dinner with them tonight!

"Well, unless the pilot is going to stop by a McDrive, then I would be delighted," I say jokingly!

Just before dinner, the hostess opens a large table in front of me, puts a tablecloth on it and brings in salt and pepper shakers and drinks just like a real restaurant. A few hours later, as I'm getting ready to sleep, they bring in an extra mattress to be placed on the now fully flat seat and prepare the bed for me.

After what has been one of my best flight experiences ever, Paul and I have finally landed in Jakarta Soekarno-Hatta Airport. We are reasonably rested thanks to the business class flight, but still a little spaced out with the time difference and the duration of the trip. However, we're only here for five days and we have lots to do so we need to get on with it!

We're picked up at the airport by our host Igor and his brother, who drive us to our hotel, the Santika BSD City Hotel in Serpong. This is about an hour or so from the airport and the weather is very hot and humid – we're not used to it.

After the rest of the day to chill out, recover a little and get a good night's sleep, we are picked up the next morning from our hotel and driven to the company's animation studio located in the BSD City area to the south-west of Jakarta. As we are driving through the various streets, we can't fail to notice the extreme differences in living conditions. As we drive out of our five-star hotel, 200 metres down the road there are a number of slums and then, a few streets later, there is an amazing shopping mall and then more slums. As we discuss that with Igor, he explains to us that BSD City – which stands for Bumi Serpong Damai – is a fully private area the size of about 10,000 football fields that has been built over the last 25 years. It is essentially private land with new modern developments for the Indonesian middle class and not everyone can afford the standards.

When we arrive at the studio, we meet the rest of their team. The studio is a large modern house that has been converted into a workplace with a few desks, a waiting area and an internal garden! At the back, there is another garden where they have built a temporary sheltered area where we are going to set up their temporary VR studio system. This will allow them to fine-tune their content and make adjustments before opening up in 2017 in a large shopping mall in the centre of Jakarta.

All the boxes arrived a week before us and we start to open everything to make sure it's all in one piece. The VR headsets we have supplied to them have been packed in a premium case and look great. (See photos page 166.)

After two days of setting up with cameras, wiring and configuring their content to work with our technology, we're all done. After a few tests, we identify a few small issues. This is essentially because the studio floor is installed on wooden floorboards that vibrate as we walk on them. Since the overall truss structure is installed on those same floorboards, the vibrations travel to the cameras via the truss and this affects the tracking. A couple of trips down to the hardware store with the team to make sure we can secure the truss strongly to the building and the problem is pretty much solved.

We have another small issue with our VR headset struggling a little with the hot and humid air in Indonesia. Both the screen and the wireless receiver emit some heat. We have a small thermal heat sink on the wireless board and a number of strategically placed cooling vents, but the air is so humid and so hot that, after a couple of hours of operation, it just overheats and shuts down.

This can be a bit of an issue, as it means the team will need a few extra headsets to help them go over a full day of operations, but it's nothing too major that we cannot deal with.

After the third day, the installation is now fully complete, tested and their content is working with the studio. We will need to do some adjustments with them over the coming weeks, but that can be done remotely. We have been very well looked after by the team. They have taken us to different restaurants, we have met their wives and children and they have shown us where they live. It is an exciting time for us as they are our first international customers, but, more importantly, they have some very exciting development plans for their VR entertainment locations. We are going to be part of it, so this is another very exciting opportunity to develop together.

On the day we check out of the hotel, we have a little panic as the receptionist hands me the bill for the five-night stay. It shows an amount of 5.7millions rupiah! I've gotten a little used to the extreme exchange difference between the UK pound and the Indonesian rupiah over the last few days. Parking fees cost around 2,000 rupiah (10 pence) and the restaurant bills come in at over 500,000-700,000 rupiahs (£30 to £40) for four of us. When I see that hotel bill with an amount of 5,786,000 at the bottom, I get a little hot under the collar while I get my phone out and use my currency convertor to work out the actual cost in British pounds! It comes to £330 . . . It's interesting that this is a five-star luxury hotel and two rooms have cost us just over £30 a night including two dinners and a couple of drinks. It's a shame James and Stan didn't come; they could have had one of their event parties on the cheap for a change!

Back onto a 20-hour trip halfway around the world. When I land in London, I use the Emirates chauffeur service included in our business flight ticket to take me to Euston Train Station where I take the train up to the Liverpool studio to meet a potential client. I then fly back the next day to arrive at base just in time for our 4th of November board meeting!

It's November now – the final month of the company. In exactly 26 days, we will be closing the doors permanently!

During that board meeting, where all five directors are present this time, we discuss the company's financial situation and how we are going to handle a recent flood we had in the studio that created several thousand pounds worth of damage.

The insurance inspector has been in and hopefully we will get some compensation.

We also discuss the Jakarta installation and one of the director / shareholders complains that we should have asked for the balance of the payment while we were on site with the client.

I did find the request a little odd, as we were not equipped to take card payments and a foreign cheque would not have been suitable. I am not going to carry £25k in cash with me. Igor has promised us that they will do a bank transfer shortly and I have no reason not to trust them. In any case, the licence we have installed is a limited temporary licence that only works for 60 days. If they don't pay, they will end up with a useless system anyway.

MY FAVORITE QUOTE

"If you can't fly then run. If you can't run, then walk. And if you can't walk, then crawl, but whatever you do, you have to keep moving forward."
Martin Luther King Jr – leader of the civil rights movement.

LESSON LEARNED:

I selected that quote specifically for this chapter as the last few months have been critical and knowing that we are on the edge of having to close the company does affect the whole team morale. However, my motto in life – whatever I do – is to never give up. So, as per this quote, I have kept going even when we got the news that there would be no more financial bailouts from the investors, even when we had the flood and even when everything looked bleak. I kept going and tried everything in my power to turn our fortunes around.

CHAPTER TWENTY THREE

Too little, too late

It is now nearly three weeks since we returned from Jakarta. The last few weeks have been focused on finishing our simulator, cleaning up the studio after the flood in the hope that we can open it to the public in order to bring in some much-needed sales, continuing to develop our VR studio and pushing for some sales leads to be finalised so we can receive deposits and buy us some time.

We have over a dozen serious leads and at least three of them should be signed any day now. We really need this as our bank account balance is melting by the day.

We have, unfortunately, not yet received the balance from Jakarta simply because there is a jittery issue with the tracking. I've had a number of conference calls with Igor and, having met the team, Paul and I know they will pay the balance. In some ways it is unfortunate that our first big sale ended up being halfway around the world, as it would be easier to help and adjust if they were nearby, but it is what it is. We are tweaking and helping to make sure the tracking works as well as it should. We've built two additional headsets and have sent them to Igor's team to allow them to handle the overheating issue.

It's the 25th of November and another one of our regular board meetings with all five directors. The meeting starts with one of the shareholders expressing his dissatisfaction at the fact that we have not been paid by the Jakarta team and repeating that he was flabbergasted that we came back from Jakarta without the payment in hand. Obviously a £25k injection into our bank account would be very welcome at this stage, so I understand the stress around it, but I also understand Igor's position. He wants the two issues resolved before settling the balance.

Paul and I have been doing a number of remote connections and have just asked the team to change the network card in their tracking server. The Vicon team has advised that there could be a bottleneck and, sure enough, this seems to have improved the jittery issue. As for the overheating headsets, we have sent them two additional ones at no extra cost so everything is in hand and will be resolved shortly. We can get payment sorted soon.

I am due to go over to France to finalise the arcade and project with the French client. I'm informed by two of the directors that this is not a wise use of company money and that there does not seem to be any purpose to the trip at this stage. I agree to defuse the situation and confirm that I will pay for the trip myself.

Another part of the meeting is an extensive review of the CNES magnetic tracking solution. During my last visit to them in August, they lent me two devices for us to test and develop with. I have been doing a bit of work on the algorithm, and our developer Frank has recently started to help me. We are trying to make sense of the algorithm to establish an accurate tracking solution.

We have made good progress, but are at the stage where we need to sign the agreement and this means committing a £50k upfront royalty payment early in the new year. There are mixed feelings as to whether we should go ahead since right now we do not have that money. Even if we can finalise one or two sales, the money will likely need to be managed carefully for a further few months.

We then review the dozens of live leads, ranging from Nebraska University to the Enterspace Museum and from Ferrari World to the New Zealand kitchen designer. We even have Mr Rankin flying in from France with his team in his private business jet to negotiate a deal to install our tech in his various entertainment locations in France.

We met him in Barcelona and have been in touch ever since. It looks like we're about to sign a deal. In total, if all of the estimates are to be signed, this will be a revenue in excess of £2million. We just need to sign a couple in the next two weeks to keep going.

Finally, we then review the business accounts that James has prepared along with a short-term forecast. There is currently just over £16,000 left on the account, we're due to receive £3,500 for our insurance claim, we still have the F1 chassis in Southampton due to go for £10,000 and, of course, the £26,000 balance from Jakarta. However, we have liabilities to Vicon for about £24,000, our staff salaries for November due shortly for £11,500, a final £5,000 for the remaining balance of our VR helmet designs and a couple of thousand pounds for small invoices.

We announce that we are going to open the studio to the public and hoping to bring in £3,000-£4,000 in December. We are also aiming to sell the small motion platform that we have used for our development, as we have some interest for it and that will bring in about £5,000 profit.

However, my small pitch detailing how we can bring in a bit of much-needed money is followed by a long silence from the two director / investors and then one of them says,
"It is too little, too late."
The state of the finances clearly show that we need to appoint a liquidator and initiate the winding-up process!

It is shocking to hear those words, but not surprising. I've known for months that our company is hanging by a thread, but my inner fighter is still there and I try to suggest some last-minute options.
"Maybe we can keep the company dormant for three months," I suggest. "This means letting all our staff go and spending a few months without any salaries for ourselves, but I'll do anything to save the company. We just need a few more weeks, just enough time to sign a couple of clients. What do you think?"

But the director / shareholders say that it is pointless. There is more rent due for the Liverpool studio in January, there are staff holidays and allowances to settle and some other liabilities due in. They say that if we make the decision to carry on and if we go completely under, the liquidators may not accept taking the company into administration. As directors, we could all be sued for any company liabilities and for mismanagement and, since these directors are also directors on other companies, they are not prepared to jeopardise their other positions.

One of the shareholders kindly says that he understands I want to save the company, but it is just too dangerous a legal position to take. The company has gone through over £1million in one year. The only thing to do is to call a Creditors' Voluntary Liquidation which will give us around 21 days' notice before it is official. If any serious monies come in before then, we have an option to stop it.

Three days later, an EGM is called, and the Creditors' Voluntary Liquidation is announced and made official. At that stage, the two director / shareholders and James make the decision to block the company bank account as it is, and no more money is to be spent.

I intervene saying that the staff salaries are due to be paid in a few days, but they rule me and Paul out and say that it will be down to the administrators to sort this out from now on.

I'm fully aware that this means the staff will not get this month's salary in the immediate future, since I expect it will take the administrators a few months to resolve. I walk out of that meeting deflated. Paul and I have a brief discussion. It is such a shame: two and half years since we formed the company. We were doing well before we accepted the huge investment – did we make a mistake? It is easy to look back and criticise the actions we took and the decisions we made but, deep down, I know the investment opportunity was a chance of a lifetime. It just didn't work out.

On the 1st of December, we call a staff meeting. I've just returned from a dentist appointment where I had an anaesthetic to numb an area of my mouth, so I'm not feeling great but I take my seat next to Paul ready to announce the terrible news to our staff.

As per the previous staff announcement regarding the Financial Rescue Plan, James is once again sitting in between two staff members crawling down his seat trying to make himself as invisible as possible. He clearly feels embarrassed about having to announce the end.

I sit there for a couple of minutes looking at James and thinking how he likes to be seen in nice clothing or in first class travel or posh hotels, but when it comes to facing the consequences (many of them due to his own actions and decisions,) he is nowhere in sight, or supportive or reassuring to staff and this kind of attitude deeply annoys me. Let's be honest, we all make mistakes in life and, as far as I am concerned, I have no problem in owning up to them, apologising and putting them right if I can. But people like James, who sneak out of their responsibilities and try to avoid the consequences of their own actions, have zero respect from me.

It is really not a pleasant thing to do to have to announce to our staff – who have been nothing but loyal and hardworking – that this is the end. It is even harder to tell them on the 1st of December with the upcoming festive season and, worse, since we know the company funds have been frozen, we are unable to pay them their November salary and will be unable to pay them their December annual leave and other dues since we will no longer be in control. The reaction from the staff is not nice – as expected. There is a lot of anger and a lot of heated discussions.

I remain as calm as I can. I feel so sorry for everyone, I feel sorry for myself, I feel sorry for our potential clients that are counting on us to deliver our tech to them, I feel sorry for Igor in Indonesia. It is such a sad day. The meeting ends with every staff member dismissed on the spot and sent home.

From the minute we sign the agreement to go into liquidation, we are no longer company directors. However, over the following three weeks, I still work hard to help staff to get the paperwork and the help they need to get their last salary from the local government salary protection fund. I also spend a lot of time with Paul to prepare the stocktake, asset lists, affidavits and documents required by the administrators. Secretly, I'm still holding onto the possibility of a change of fortune with some sales coming in, but if not I'm going to work as hard as I can to make the administration process as smooth as possible and make sure everyone get paid and that things are cleaned up properly.

A few days later, we all receive official notification that the liquidation meeting will be held on the 22nd of December. We are required to attend in order to go over the company finances and status and to sign our directorship over.

MY FAVORITE QUOTE

"Our greatest weakness lies in giving up. The most certain way to succeed is always to try just one more time."
Thomas Edison – entrepreneur and inventor.

LESSON LEARNED:

That's it, another similar quote to reinforce my way in life of never giving up no matter what.

However, regardless how strongly one can feel about not giving up, sometimes there is no choice. Sometimes we are forced to give up as this is the only right thing to do. Even if your heart tells you not to give up, the head has got to be the strongest and make the right decision to stop.

I didn't want to put the company into administration. We're so close to signing a few more clients and our F1 simulator is pretty much ready. It's so unfair to be so close and yet giving up. But the shareholders are right, it would be risky to continue. When that "give up" decision comes after trying, trying again and trying one more time, then at least there is the comfort that the best has been attempted.

CHAPTER TWENTY-FOUR

The truth is out

The next couple of weeks leading to the liquidation meeting are still very busy. We have to provide lots of information to the liquidators, such as the exact list of creditors, access to the complete list of company documents, a list of potential people who we feel may be interested in purchasing the company and we have to prepare our affidavits and plans for the potential future of the company.

I have remained in constant contact with Igor in Indonesia to help him fine-tune his system and iron out any bugs. We've decided not to inform him of the situation just yet in case it can be turned around and also to make sure he does not withhold the balance payment. As you will see in the next and final chapter, Igor is a true, genuine, honest individual and a great businessman. Even after he knew the company was in administration, once the problem had been resolved he offered to pay the full balance.

I have also been busy relaunching my own freelance software development company for which, aside from fixed incomes and small jobs for existing clients, I have not taken any development work for 12 months. It is a little daunting, as I have been on the development scene locally for over five years before slowing down to focus on this company and I have built a reasonably good reputation. I now have to start putting my name around again and letting people know that I'm available for freelance work.

As mentioned earlier in this book, James wanted me to shut down my software development company (for good reasons,) but I am now glad that I did not. Now I can switch back to work on this and get some development work as quickly as possible. Aside from the money Paul and I invested personally in the company, as well as the reduced salary we have taken for the last five months combined with the fact that as directors of the company we are not covered by the local government salary protection fund, we are not going to get a salary for November and December or any of our holiday pay. It's not a great position to be in.

About a week before the liquidation meeting is due to take place, we have a brief ex-director / shareholder meeting to discuss the liquidation process, review our affidavits on what exactly we feel happened that lead to this liquidation and what to expect next. We also review whether there has been any progress with sales that could alter the now pretty much inevitable liquidation. Sadly, the couple of sales that are about to be signed up are delayed because it is December. I'm sure you have probably noticed, but there seems to be a general "non-business mood" in August and December of every year where most people postpone decisions and actions to either September once the summer holidays are over with or to January once the festive holidays are over with. This, sadly, does not play in our favour as we know we are days away from signing at least one or two more clients who will pay their 50% deposit. This would be more than sufficient to stop the liquidation process, but, since these clients have decided to wait, this just hammers the final nails into the company's coffin.

We have continued to answer the company's emails and phone calls while informing the liquidators of the processes and running any decisions via them first in order to make sure everything is done officially and properly. We did this firstly with the slight hope that we might be able to turn things around at the last hour with a good sales income. In any case, even if the process is inevitable, I feel we have a duty to make sure the company is wound down as cleanly and as professionally as possible. This is to keep the highest possible value in it, whether it is fully wound down or whether it is going to be sold and started again by someone else. With a high value, all creditors would be paid up and shareholders would get some of their investment back. Hopefully, since it has so many opportunities, someone will be interested in taking it over and continuing the work done so far.

At that brief meeting, James informs all of us that he is unfortunately not able to attend the liquidation meeting on the 22nd as he booked his family holiday weeks ago and is flying out the day before. One of the shareholders asks him if he can delay this by a couple of days and join his family later as it is important that he attends this meeting. James says that, as it is a long-haul flight, it is not ideal to let his family fly by themselves. It is agreed that Stan will represent James at the liquidation meeting! Of course at this time, we have no reason to suspect anything, but, as you will read in a few paragraphs, after the quite unexpected liquidation meeting ends, all of us ask ourselves the question, "Was this holiday really planned in advance? Or could it really not have been altered slightly?" To this day, we can't help think that considering the turn of events at the liquidation meeting, James really made sure by any means possible that he was not going to be there. It was safer for him . . .

It's Thursday the 22nd of December 2016. We're only three days away from Christmas and even though I'm not a dreamer, there is a slight part of me that somehow is hoping for a Christmas miracle that might change things around at the last minute. On that day, we certainly do all get a big surprise, but it's not the kind of surprise we want.

At the meeting, there are most of our creditors who have been invited to hear the liquidation process and confirm their claim. There are all five ex-directors except James who is represented in person by Stan and there is also one of our other smaller non-director shareholders.

The liquidators introduce themselves and the agenda for the meeting. We do not know at the beginning, but the meeting is going to take six hours in total. Firstly, there's a recap of the company's structure. By law, the five different limited companies that make up the structure are going to be liquidated one by one because they are treated as single companies with no specific relation between them. Then, there is a list of the total amount of money owed to creditors. This now comes to just over £65k which includes £24k to Vicon and about £26k in staff and director salaries and holidays. The remaining creditors, who total up to about £15k, are the designer working on our VR helmets, who is owed around £5k; a couple of local guys who helped with some of our content design, who are owed about £2k; there is £2k of rent on our studio; a social security bill for about £3k; and then about another 12 individuals or companies that are owed between £200 and £800.

Of course, we have £16k in the company bank account that is locked and has not been touched for about a month now. We are due to receive just over £3k from our insurance claim and, of course, the £25k balance from Jakarta, so our total creditor amount outstanding is about £21k. There are also administrator invoices to settle, but, considering the company assets, trademarks, patents pending and technology, we are pretty confident that this will easily be covered and that there will be a lot of money returned to the initial shareholders. While they are set to lose a fair bit, this should hopefully be limited damages to them and all creditors, staff and anybody who has been involved with the company should be paid up – albeit a little late. - However, this was not to be . . .

The first company to be liquidated is the original one Paul and I formed and since there are no commitments, no revenue and no invoices tied to that company, it is a very quick and simple process.

The second company to be liquidated is Vizuality Services. This company was set up to essentially raise all clients' invoices and settle all supplier orders. This is the main one where all the money due will be sent and where all creditors are currently listed as per above. This is also the company with which all the assets we purchased are associated. According to the recent stock list Paul and I have provided to the administrators, we have in excess of £350k of assets which we estimate to be worth around £200k at second-hand value. Some of it is still-new circuit boards and components and tracking cameras that have hardly been used.

When the decision to wind down was made back at the end of November, James sent Frank and Stan on a Liverpool round trip to collect all 20 tracking cameras, wireless headsets and some of the technology we had installed in the Liverpool studio.. They left behind the computers, server and a few other bits they couldn't carry, but that quick round trip brought back around £50k worth of assets, which are now part of the Vizuality Services assets.

The next company to be liquidated is Vizuality Studios which is – if I recall correctly as I've never fully grasped the whole structure purpose – designed to handle all our planned worldwide studio installation and franchise distribution. Since so far, we've only had our home studio and one other studio in Liverpool, which for some unknown reason ended up being under the Vizuality UK company, this company has no assets, no studios, no liabilities and no revenue, so this is another easy quick wind down. Talking of the Liverpool studio, it is under a UK company structure and has no income and only has liabilities so far which account for £10k in rent and local tax. It's shortly due for another quarterly rent, which brings this to about £20k and it is under a three-year lease. Because of this, the administrators do not want to take this company, so it will have to be liquidated under a different UK-based liquidator. Since Paul and I decided to never sign those directorship forms back in July, I am now delighted to not have that burden to deal with as well.

I feel sorry for the Liverpool studio landlord. I only met him once at the beginning of the year, so did not know him much as James has been dealing with him directly. However, considering that the technology left at the Liverpool studio is probably worth around £10k new, so maybe £6k at resale, he is not going to get much of his rent arrears back, nor will he ever receive any rent for the duration of the signed lease. As of today, I do not know what happened to the Liverpool studio. I know the UK company was wound down nearly a year later, but I don't know if James ended up being liable for any of the outstanding money or whether it all got written off.

Next is Vizuality Design. This company is where our two patent-pending technology, registrations, brand and logo trademarks and all our content and development are registered under. This is essentially designed to have all our IP (intellectual property) under one company. The shareholders asked me and Paul recently how much we feel the technology we have developed over the last two years could be worth. We responded that it would be difficult to put a price on this as, at the end of the day, it is worth what an investor is prepared to pay based on the potential value it can generate in the future. However, we have successfully built one of the only two wireless VR headsets available in the world at the time. We now have a 95% completed F1 racing simulator with a unique VR helmet and there is nothing else like that in the world. The company brand has been promoted around the world and is now well known in the VR industry from Shanghai to San Francisco. We have three VR contents nearly completed. We have over 20 good sales leads with a few of them about to be signed. Considering all of this, and the fact that our agreements with BroadMesse,

Attraktion and the CNES, we feel that the company's IP could be worth a couple of million. But, as I said earlier, it is worth whatever someone is prepared to pay for it. Investors are only going to pay for a genuine, above board and fully registered intellectual property – and that is the problem!

As the administrator announces the liquidation process of Vizuality Design, he marks it down as having no assets, no revenue and no liabilities, so it's not worth anything and is about to be simply wound down.

"Hold on!" shouts one of our investors while standing up. "You cannot value that company at nothing. There is intellectual property registered in that company, there are trademarks and content. This is worth lots of money!"

"No, I'm afraid it is not," responds the administrator. "We have checked all documents for the company and there are no official registrations or trademarks, there are no patent-pending applications and the copyrighted content is not worth anything by itself."

As we all stand still in silence trying to grasp what the administrator has just said, our shareholder continues to query how he came to that conclusion. He explains that they reviewed all the documents we provided, they ran some official searches on the different patent registrars and trademarks and there were not even any applications made or processed.

I won't describe the "interesting" language used by our angry shareholders, but they – and Paul and I – feel we have just been dealt a huge blow! What happened to the meetings discussing the importance of the registration of our IP? What happened to the detailed drawings and listings of our technology that we provided to James? What happened to the company name registration and, more importantly, what happened to the large sum of money we paid to our lawyers who, according to James, had been handling this?

More importantly still – although this did not become clear until a few days after the meeting – without any IP registered, our company and our technology was worthless to any investors. An overwhelming sense of fear dawns on us as we realise this means we would never had passed the due diligence process even if we had accepted offers from our investment opportunities. Maybe this is the reason why MerciaTech never responded to us.

So, as you can appreciate, the frustration that Paul and I feel after having worked so hard on developing our technology is indescribable. It feels that all the hard work – hundreds and hundreds of hours of work – the stress and the travelling around the world to attend events was all pointless and a waste of time!

Equally – from the investors' side – having trusted our company with a large amount of their money means that the hope of any potential value that could have been raised out of the intellectual property has been wiped out in an instant. A company that could have potentially been worth a few hundred thousands of pounds at minimum – and up to a couple of million at best – is now worth a big fat zero!

It is also worth noting that since we cannot fulfil our part of the agreement with the CNES, I am asked to return the two sample devices that were lent to us for development purposes. The inventor of the technology subsequently continued the application for his patent on his own and that patent was granted under number FR3035718A1 in May 2017!

As you can see, as mentioned at the beginning of this book, we worked hard, we developed some amazing tech and created some insane opportunities, but that did not matter. Without the IP registered, we were never going to be investable and that means we would have never been able to grow as planned.

Now, if you think this was bad from James, that wasn't the last of our surprises. After a few hours in this liquidation meeting, we reach the last company, Vizuality Ltd. The administrator announces that the company has no assets, no revenue and liabilities of around £660,000 which is the whole loan note agreements from our shareholder / investors with the initial amount having been invested in return for shares. However, since the loan notes are on an insecure basis, they will be written off and the company will be wound down!

The same investor who raised his voice to query the IP issue earlier in the meeting stands up once again, sending his chair flying back with a bang on the floor, saying,

"What? Is this a joke?" The administrator responds,

"No. The loan notes have been agreed with this company; however, the money to purchase the assets, pay staff and all other travel and marketing expenses has been spent with Vizuality Services and those are two different companies and are treated as such in the eyes of the law."

"But, come on! It is obvious that all the money spent in Vizuality Services comes from that investment and loan notes in Vizuality Ltd," responds the investor.

"Yes of course," agrees the administrator. "But there are no transfer agreements in place, so as far as the law is concerned, the money received in one company and the money spent in the other cannot be linked to each other even if they are one and the same."

Now, please excuse me if I did not explain the exact terms and reasons for the above, as I am not that good with agreements and complex structures as I mentioned earlier. What is clear, though, is that whatever James instructed our lawyers to do and whatever agreements were drafted and signed by the investors were clearly not right. This means that they now had no option to be on the list of creditors to be owed money from any liquidation proceeds unless someone was prepared to purchase the whole lot for one good sum of money.

So here we are. It's the end of the liquidation meeting and we're all very saddened by the way the events have turned out. I still had hopes when I woke up that morning that our company – our baby – could be turned around, that it could be valued at a decent price, that all creditors could be paid promptly and that an investor could see the opportunity and buy into it and we could start afresh and continue where we left off. But this time, it was not going to be.

It's no wonder James was not at that meeting!

Paul and I wondered afterwards what would have happened if he had been there. While he may have genuinely made a mistake with the loan note agreements, he obviously knew about the IP issue, so I would have liked to be able to ask him for a reason as to why no registrations or patents had ever been processed. What was he thinking? Surely, as a financial investor, he would have known that the company was never going to be able to secure any decent investments without a proper portfolio of IP in place.

MY FAVORITE QUOTE

"No more romanticising about how cool it is to be an entrepreneur. It's a struggle to save your company's life – and your own skin – every day of the week."
Spencer Fry – co-founder of Carbonmade.

LESSON LEARNED:

This is so true for the majority of start-ups in the first couple of years of their life. Once a company is established, things get a little easier, although there are always some ups and downs that are going to be challenging. In our case, however, our first year was made so much harder than it needed to be – and all of it for nothing.

CHAPTER TWENTY FIVE

The end

After the liquidation meeting ends, I continue to work for a couple of months in full collaboration with the administrators in order to assist Igor and his team with their integration and provide assistance they would have expected as a client of the company.

In early January, Igor offers to settle the balance payment; however, the licence we gave them initially on the tracking system was a temporary licence so in order to continue using their tracking software they need a new permanent licence – which only Vicon can issue. As they are, of course, aware of the liquidation process and are owed £24k, they ask for their overdue invoice to be paid before issuing the permanent licence.

Unfortunately, due to legal requirements, the administrators inform us that they are not able to favour one creditor over another. As such, they cannot at this stage pay the money owed to Vicon, even though it would have been enough with the balance paid by Igor.

I try to find a solution and even try to negotiate a deal with Vicon – all with the administrators' approval, but none are accepted. Eventually, Igor manages to purchase a licence from an Asian Vicon retailer and, in turn, says that he is not going to pay the balance since he has to purchase it somewhere else.

In February, Igor and his brother fly into London for another project they are working one and they invite me to go and have dinner with them. We have a great evening, we discuss the whole process and they fully understand and confirm that they appreciate that I remain committed to them and continue to help even though I am not getting paid for it.

The reason I do it is out of pure guilt. At the end of the day, these guys are the first ones to trust us with their money and purchase the technology we worked so hard to build. The turn of events for the company were very unfair on them so, by assisting them afterwards, they

manage to get a working studio at least. I know
they actually launched a few months later for an
initial three-month event.

Afterwards, an invitation of offers is made by
the administrators and is sent to several possible
interested parties. It seems, however, that the
lack of IP and the disastrous handling of the
company finances means that, as far as we are
aware, only a handful of offers are received. The
administrators accept the highest offer, which
we find out later is from one of our original
investors who purchases all the assets with a
view to reselling them and getting some profit
back.

Once the sale of the company is confirmed by
the administrators, it then takes several months
for anything to be finalised. Our staff eventually
end up being paid by the safety fund, albeit
several months late and not in full.

So that's it. That's been my story for the last
couple of years! It has been one crazy ride and I
have now fully returned to my original freelance
software development and I am delighted that I
have managed to restore my reputation quickly
and have been busier than ever. I will always
remember my time at Vizuality as the
opportunity of a lifetime and, while it did not
work out, I do feel that I tried my very best and,
as such, I have no regrets. Yes, of course, there

are many things I would do differently if I had the opportunity of hindsight, but wouldn't we all do that for many things in life if we could?

For a little while after stopping Vizuality, I remained committed to VR. I kept well informed on the technology available, kept abreast of what our previous competitors were up to and consulted on projects with a couple of clients who wanted some advice on VR arcades.

However, I now have little involvement with VR, aside from visiting the occasional exhibition and trying out various VR equipment. I am no longer developing VR content or hardware.

It is with interest that I regularly look back on what we were working on and I assess where we would be at today if we had managed to stay afloat a little longer! One thing that I'm pretty sure of is that our wireless headset would not have been a great success. You see, back then our wireless headset had a resolution of 1920 pixelsx1080 pixels at a frequency of 60 frames per seconds. Without sounding too technical, that is around 125million pixels to transmit between the computer and the headset every second!

At the time, we were already working on our next gen headset which would have had an increased resolution of 2440 pixelsx1200 pixels, bringing the bandwidth usage to around 176million pixels every second. However, the game-changer in VR came with the increase in the frame per second. You see, the faster the screen refreshes, the lower the latency is and the – new at the time – but now 90 frame per second (FPS) standard is a must in any current VR headset.

As of today, the maximum number of pixels we are able to transfer with existing technology is around 330million, which is nearly three times the amount our original headset needed. This is good enough to provide a resolution similar to the Oculus Rift CV1; however, having tested that technology, it is quite unstable and unreliable. The problem is that, being the maximum currently possible, it is already redundant as new headsets coming out on the market have a resolution far higher.

As an example, one of my favourite VR headsets currently on the market – as far as resolution / quality is concerned – is the Samsung Odyssey+ with a resolution of 1440 pixelsx1600 pixels per eye at 90 FPS. This is over 410million pixels refreshing every second – and there are even higher resolution headsets available now.

The only suitable wireless technology that is currently in use today and can handle this type of bandwidth is the high frequency – 60Ghz –

range. This is the one we started with, but, as we quickly found out, it is not suitable for multiplayer arcades as it is subject to line of sight as well as interferences.

So, I guess, like VRcade – our other wireless headset competitor – we would have ended up switching to using backpack computers to drive wired headsets for the players.

As for tracking in VR, up until recently optical tracking solution has been the only way possible. The problem, as mentioned, is the huge cost involved. I have tested several times the technology of a new small company that has been developing their own custom optical tracking system and, while they have some really good tech, after about two years of being around and developing, they are still not quite there (as of April 2019) when it comes to having a suitable working solution to track multiple users over a large area of 100 square metre (1075 square feet) or more.

The latest tech is the arrival of inside out tracking which does not require any external tracking equipment. The headset is able to position the user in the room with accuracy. It is, however, not designed to track a user over a large area, as there is a drift that builds up quickly which reports inaccurate positions.

However, I've recently had the opportunity to test the development from a company that got set up just as our company was winding down. They have developed something pretty amazing which is able to track dozens of players over a very large area in excess of 1,000 square metres without any problems at all.

As for our F1 simulator, I do miss it. I've seen and tried lots of other simulators, but I am yet to try something that came close to what we developed.

So, this is it for my story. I wrote this book as I felt it was a good time for me to do so. For a while, I had mixed feelings and a fair bit of resentment at James for messing it all up, but, as time has gone by, I've changed. Yes, James did do a lot wrong (and speaking for myself, I made a number of mistakes as well) but, on the other hand, James was a gambler and he hoped that by being extravagant and presenting the company as the new VR company to watch, he would quickly draw attention to us and raise lots of investment opportunities. As you've seen in the book, it worked! So, whether James was right or wrong, I'm pretty sure that a lot of readers would disagree one way or the other.

Many successful companies that have made it big have done so by the skin of their teeth and by gambling big, not by peacefully waiting for things to happen. With hindsight, the only big mistake James made was to not make sure the company's intellectual property was registered properly. Aside from that, whether James was right or wrong is more of a personal view on running an international business. As far as I am concerned, there were a number of things very early on that I was not happy with. I had the power to call an EGM and I had the power to say "stop!" If I had, things may have been different, but I didn't until July and by then it was too late. So, ultimately, it is equally my fault that the company failed. I should have been stronger and I should have been more assertive much earlier.

I sincerely hope you have found it interesting, but, more importantly, I hope it has provided you with some experiences you may be able to use or refer to if you ever start your own company. If you have any comments, please feel free to contact me on the website at 1b1m1y.com

I will end this book with three more quotes instead of one, as I could not choose between them.

Thank you for reading my story.

THREE MORE FAVORITE QUOTES

"I knew that if I failed, I wouldn't regret that, but I knew the one thing I might regret is not trying."
Jeff Bezos – founder and CEO of Amazon.

"Success is not final; failure is not fatal. It is the courage to continue that counts."
Winston S Churchill – British Prime Minister during World War II.

"A man can fall many times in life, but he's never a failure until he refuses to get back up."
Evel Knievel – American stunt performer and entertainer.

1b1m1y.com

1 Business, 1 Million, 1 Year

Printed in Great
Britain
by Amazon

31128925R00183